Transgender Tales

Adventures and Misadventures
On a Journey from Transvestite to
Transsexual

By

Helen Dale

© Helen Dale 2018

All rights reserved. No part of this publication may be reproduced or transmitted in any form or by any means, electronic, mechanical, including photocopying, recording or by any information storage retrieval system without permission for the author.

The right of Helen Dale to be identified as the author of this work has been asserted by her in accordance with the Copyright, Designs and Patents Act 1988

The Wedding, The Demonstration and The Dream are fiction and any similarity to actual people or organisations is purely coincidental.

Tranzcare
www.helendaleauthor.info
info@tranzcare.info
https://www.facebook.com/helendaleauthor/

ISBN   9781999632915

Introduction

This book is a collection of a diary I kept between 1997 and 1999 when I moved to Salford and had a number of Trans people stay at my flat and go to Manchester's gay village; some short stories (originally published in Northern Concord's magazine "Crosstalk" under the name Helen Williamson), a poem "Can You Tell Me What I Am?" together and other humorous anecdotes.

At the start of this period, I identified as transvestite — but, over the following few years I started to question whether that was appropriate or if I was actually transsexual. It includes coming out to two of my oldest friends as well as my (then) wife and daughter and other family members.

I hope you enjoy it. If so, you may like to buy my autobiography *"A Tale of Two Lives (A funny Thing Happened on the Way to the Palace) available on Amazon and in other outlets* **ISBN** 978-1-9996329-7-7 (paperback) 978-1-9996329-9-1 (hardcover)

Check out my other books too listed at the back of this volume and follow my Helen Dale Author facebook page for latest information:

https://www.facebook.com/helendaleauthor/

Please note that the term "tranny" is used throughout much of this book; that was a common term at the time of writing and whilst it is considered inappropriate by many trans people these days, I've retained it as it was how many of us identified.

Helen Dale

February 2018

(updated to correct some grammatical and spelling errors and update the list of other books – March 2022)

Contents

The Wedding 5
Close Shaves & other incidents
or: Been there, done that, got the T shirt/ Blouse! 8
Ms Dale's Diary 10
The Demonstration 66
Fair Cop 68
The Dream 69
Can You Tell Me What I Am 72
Coming Out 1 — Mission Impossible 77
    The "Briefing Papers" 78
    Preliminary briefing notes 78
    Preamble 78
    Stage 2 Briefing Notes — Mission Limitations 78
    Briefing Notes — The Secret? 79
    Stage 4 — The Revelation 80
Coming Out 2 — At Work 83
Coming Out 3 — to Jo and Jenny 84
Read it and Weep 85
So don't believe me! 85
Other incidents 87

The Wedding

(This was written years before the Gender Recognition & Civil Partnership Acts)

"Blushing Bride - and So She Might", screamed the headlines in the Sunday Scandal. "Christine James married Peter Walker on Thursday, but the blushing bride has a secret. She was CHRISTOPHER James before undergoing a sex change operation in 1993! And the registry office wedding was illegal because regardless of surgery, she is still legally a man. No doubt she will be blushing even more when the police call to see her!"

The editor pulled a bottle of whisky out of his bottom draw and poured a slug into a plastic cup which he handed to the reporter who had followed up an anonymous tip off leading to the latest story.

"Well done, Nick, That's the ticket. Our readers will love it. I'll put it on page 6, can't fit it in earlier because of the Royal revelations."

Two days later, the editor called Nick to his office again.

"That story about the sex change bride. You are sure you got it right, aren't you?" He demanded.

"Absolutely, I checked out her history. Born 1955 and registered as a male, lived as Christopher until the sex change in 1993. Why?"

"We've had a writ from her solicitors for libel, that's why. And, what's more, the police don't seem to be taking any action against her."

"They haven't got a leg to stand on, chief. The facts speak for themselves. The police are probably just dragging their feet. In fact, that could be a follow up story - maybe the officer responsible has some reason for taking no action which he wouldn't like revealed!"

"Good idea, check it out".

Later that week, the reporter knocked on his editor's door.

"That sex change wedding story. Turns out that the copper involved was a transvestite who retired from the force the day after filing a "no further action recommended" report on the case."

"Fan-bloody-tastic! Did you get any pics of the copper in drag by any chance?"

"Not yet. He's disappeared from sight for the moment".

"Well, keep digging. In the meantime, let's run this as the second lead on the front page."

"Great! Any news about the writ?"

"Yeah. Strange that. They're still claiming damages for alleging that the wedding was illegal when they say it wasn't. Counsel thinks they may be planning to use it as a test case in the European Court."

With no trace of the police officer and no further developments, the story died and other scandals took its place in the scurrilous paper.

Finally, the date of the hearing arrived and the editor and reporter joined their legal advisors at the court.

"Let's go over the facts once more." the bewigged barrister in his long robe suggested. "There is no possibility of incorrect identification, the bride "Christine" was registered as male at birth and lived in that role until undergoing gender reassignment surgery, she then changed her name by deed poll and under that name married Peter Walker. I really cannot see what their defence could possibly be. Regardless of her sex change, she is still legally male and two males may not marry."

Counsel for the plaintiffs presented their claim for damages arising from the incorrect assertion that Christine and Peter's marriage had been illegal. It was then the defendant's turn to question Christine.

"Your name is now Christine James, but you were previously Christopher James. Is that correct?" demanded the barrister.

"No, it is not correct" Christine replied. "My name is now Christine Walker, not James."

"But you were formally known as Christopher James?" insisted the barrister, irritated at the original response.

"That is correct." replied Christine.

"And you were registered at birth as a male?"

"Yes."

"Then, in the eyes of the law, you are male."

"Yes, but...."

The barrister cut her off and asked his next question "And you are aware that it is illegal for two males to marry in this country."

"In this country, yes. Other countries are more civilised about these matters."

"We are not concerned with other countries. As your wedding was illegal, the newspaper was quite within its rights to publicise the truth and there can be no claim against it. No further questions. I submit, my Lord that it is quite obvious that there is no case for my clients to answer and ask for the case to be dismissed with costs awarded against the plaintiff."

The judge looked up over his glasses at Christine and James' barrister. "Do you have any further relevant evidence to present?" he asked.

"Yes, my Lord. I would like Peter Walker to take the stand."

"Are you certain that this is going to be relevant? I will not have my court used as a soap box for propaganda purposes."

"It is highly relevant my Lord."

"Very well, continue."

Peter walked across to the witness box, five feet seven tall of slight build, he had a smooth complexion and sported a narrow moustache.

"Your name is Peter Walker, is that correct?"

"Yes sir"

"But it wasn't always "Peter" Walker, was it?"

"No, I was registered as Patricia at birth and it was only when I decided to live as a male at the age of nineteen that I adopted the name Peter. Christine and I met at a transsexual support group. We fell in love and decided to get married after we'd both had our operations."

"So, legally, you are still a female and as Christine is male, your wedding is legal?"

"Of course, but the newspaper was just interested in a bit of scandal."

The editor turned to his reporter. "You're fired!" he whispered angrily.

The libel award did not break records but was still substantial. The judge accepted that the notoriety resulting from the libel would add to the difficulties both Christine and Peter faced in trying to find work.

But, the problems for the Sunday Scandal didn't end with the judge's award.

As he left the court, the editor was approached by the Walker's solicitor accompanied by a tall, well dressed, lady.

"I believe that you have been looking for me," the woman said. "I was Detective Inspector Childs until I took early retirement which enabled me to undergo surgery. Your newspaper alleged that it was because I was a transvestite that I did not proceed with the case against the Walkers. That was libellous."

The solicitor handed the editor another writ. "I suggest that you consider settling this one out of court" he suggested.

Close Shaves & other incidents
or: Been there, done that, got the T shirt/ Blouse!

I hope the following items don't give the impression that I'm boasting about my exploits - well, maybe I am, but maybe too, they will help to show that you can survive most incidents when dressed without it becoming a total disaster.

First time out in public

My first time out in public It must have been about 1963 - or thereabouts (I can't honestly remember now - but I would have been about 16). I'd been dressing since before my teens; first in my sister's clothes, then my mothers and anything else I found in the piles of stuff left for scout jumble sales. But this was my first real outing in public.

I was living in Suffolk at the time and took a bus to the local railway station, then caught a train to London. This meant changing at Cambridge onto the main line. Mainline UK trains in those days tended to use corridor coaches with toilets at each end which were not overlooked by other passengers in the compartments. So, it was relatively easy to slip into one of these toilets and get changed while the train was moving. I then timed my exit to coincide with another stop - so that it looked as though I had just got on - rather than let people wonder where I had been since leaving Cambridge.

At Liverpool Street Station in London, I took the underground to Piccadilly Circus in the heart of the west end and walked around the shops. Nobody took any notice of me - but, then, in those days transvestism was virtually unheard of.

On the way home, I was going to change again in the toilets on the train when a ticket inspector called to me - I thought I was in trouble so ran to the next carriage and used the toilet there; I changed back into my male things as quickly as I could and emerged to find the inspector coming along the corridor - he only wanted to check that I had a valid ticket.

This might have put me off using trains for a long time - if not dressing at all! But it didn't.

In fact, trains, and railway stations, became one of my favourite places for changing.

Change Here for ......

The traditional railway cry took on a new meaning for me when I moved to London on leaving home. I soon found out that certain railway stations had ladies' toilets which could, with care, be entered without any problem. The stations were on suburban lines and with frequent trains and few ladies used the facilities. If there was any doubt about whether there was anyone inside, a coin rolled under the outside door gave me the excuse to look inside and check if the coast was clear! If it was, then a few moments would see me inside one of the cubicles where I could take my time changing.

This was in addition to the corridor train toilets, of course, which were unisex. I soon found out which train routes had a first stop about 30 minutes out of London.

On the Southern Region, the trains were usually single compartments with access to each only from the platforms at stations - so if I had one of these to myself then I could change between stations. The main problem on these routes was that stops were rarely more than 10 - 15 minutes apart. I tended to have my feminine things on underneath a jacket and trousers - then quickly slip these off and put on my wig and a minimal amount of make-up - just enough to allow me to walk straight into the ladies' toilets and finish off. In fact, I became so proficient at this that I could do it in the four minutes it took to travel from Waterloo to Vauxhall! I knew exactly where the ladies were at Vauxhall and which compartment would stop opposite the door to the toilets.

On the Beach

(If that sounds familiar, you may just be almost as old as I am). Thirty odd years ago, when I was a young girl of about 18 - a lot slimmer and just a little more foolish I bought an orange bikini from Gorringe's department store (long since defunct) on Buckingham Palace Road London. What's foolish about that? Nothing I guess - but I did actually go on to a secluded beach near Bournemouth and went swimming in it then sunbathed! OK the nearest other people were about 100 yards away! This incident inspired a novel that I am currently writing called "Summer Dreams".

Ms Dale's Diary

If you pick up on that title, you are probably as old as me. That radio programme Mrs Dale's Diary was the bane of my life as a child. I've left the original first names in place with a few exceptions as they have already been published and, in any case; don't specifically identify the individuals concerned.

VC UK was an off-shoot of an American internet club for trans people presenting a positive image. I think we took it a step further by holding fairly frequent get-togethers for several years. NC was Northern Concorde a Transgender support network in Manchester.

Early 1997

March 14th - 15th Blackpool with VC UK Lisa's report on Blackpool I had been to Lynda's a couple of times before and had met Stephanie and gone out with her and Lynda to the Flying Handbag pub and onto Flamingo's nightclub - so I knew the probable arrangements for the VC UK visit would be to get there early evening; have a meal at the guest house - head for the Flying Handbag about 10 before going round the corner to Flamingo's.

As I lived in Manchester - an hour's drive from Blackpool, I decided I'd have a bath at my flat; get dressed in casual clothes for the drive; then change and redo my make up at Lynda's. This would make one less girl competing for the bath at the guest house. I reckoned that if I left Manchester about 6.30, I'd be in plenty of time.

As it happens, I checked my e-mails just before I was due to leave in case there were any last-minute changes of arrangements for the weekend. There were not, but there was an awful message from a friend of mine who had just had a crisis when her wife had come home unexpectedly to find her dressed! I felt I had to stop and answer her message before leaving. This meant I didn't get away from the flat until after 7. But that was OK, I'd still be in Blackpool before 8.30 - quite early enough. WRONG.

I got to the guest house just after 8.15. It was closed. No response whatsoever to ringing the bell! Nobody in!

I waited in the rain for 30 minutes; then returned to my car; drove it round to the front of the guesthouse and parked and waited ..... and waited ....and waited.

At about 9.45 I realised that they had not all just popped out for a few minutes before coming back to get read to hit the town. They were already out there!

OK. I knew there was a major TG event on at a hotel - but hadn't the faintest idea which one. I was fairly certain, however, that the others would eventually end up at Flamingos, perhaps calling at the Flying Handbag on the way.

I headed for the Flying Handbag. Remember I'd toned myself down for the drive - so was not exactly glammed up for a disco! Fortunately, my long raincoat (more of the raincoat tomorrow) meant I could slip off my long skirt and pull on a shorter one without anyone noticing! (Mind you, my short skirts are probably longer than most of the VC UK girl's longest ones).

I spent an hour or so in the Flying Handbag - got chatting to a couple of other girls - and made periodic phone calls to the guest house. Eventually I got through! The others were en route to Flamingos.

I popped round the corner, went in, ordered something to eat as I was starving having missed my expected meal at Lynda's.

Eventually I saw a familiar figure climbing the stairs - Stephanie!

United with my fellow members of VC UK and Lynda; and having checked that I did have a bed for the night; I was able to get on with enjoying what was left of the evening.

The next morning some of the girls decided to head for the pleasure beach and ride a particularly horrendous sounding rollercoaster! I had visions of wigs falling off as it looped the loop and bra fillers exploding with negative G. I wanted to see if I could find a suitable skirt for that evening so I decided I'd join the rest who were going into town en drab to do some shopping. The intrepid trio (?) went there way and the rest of us (6 guys en drab and me dressed in a suitable toned-down outfit covered by a long trenchcoat which had fitted until I lost 28lbs) headed for the town centre.

I suspect that the others were actually less comfortable than I was about me being dressed - maybe they didn't particularly want to be seen with a tranny!

As Lisa reports on her pages, we called in at a joke shop so that Sam could buy a wig; goodness only knows what the girl behind the counter thought when the others started trying to get Sam to try it on - with me standing there in the shop as well!

We also went into British Home Stores so the other girls could replenish their supplies of stockings and tights.

It was SO embarrassing being with all these men examining the nylons! I really didn't know which way to turn!

After a quick meal in a pub, we headed back to the guest house.

Oh yes, the raincoat. In Lisa's report she remarks that she isn't sure whether my raincoat is reminiscent more of Marlene Dietrich or Columbo!

HUMPH!

Saturday April 12th The VC UK had arranged to meet up in Manchester. In the end, there were only the four of us who actually made it Lisa, Samantha, Jayne and myself; as this was not too many to cope with, I invited them to stay at my flat. But with the proviso that Tina Turner wigs were banned (I didn't want them scaring the neighbour's cat).

Suitably toned down - well as toned down as Lisa and Sam can ever be - we left the flat and made our way the 100 yards or so to Lisa's car and headed for the Village.

Our first stop was Via Fosse for a meal.

There are some who claim this is the best eating place in the Village. Don't get me wrong, the decor and atmosphere are great but it is only since my personal favourite, the Blue Cafe, closed down, that I agree with this viewpoint.

After a pleasant enough meal, we walked round to my regular haunt of Paddy's Goose - where we stayed until the staff threw us out! (They only do that so that THEY can go on to Napoleons themselves!)

Which is where we headed!

The evening went well until it was time for us to go - then Lisa slipped on a patch of beer and hurt her shoulder - reactivating an old motorcycling injury. Outside Nap's, Sam, Lisa and I resigned ourselves to about an hour's wait for a taxi - but we hadn't reckoned on Jayne's powers of persuasion! She sauntered across the road and started chatting to another TV in a car. A few minutes later she beckoned us over "Come on, we've got a lift". The fact that the poor girl had been planning to head in exactly the opposite direction didn't matter at all! What Jayne said or promised I'll never know! But we gratefully accepted the "offer" and were back at the flat a few minutes later.

Saturday 26th April Sam had phoned me during the week to say that she would like to come over - so, as usual, we headed for the Village.

There was a sprinkling of regulars in Paddy's plus a couple sitting with us who seemed quite fascinated by us. Eventually, the girl (Sharon) came and sat next to me. Pointing at Sam, she said "I can see Samantha is a TV - but are you? Or are you a real woman?" Well, you can imagine I felt like a million dollars!

Alice and her partner, Maria, were also in Paddy's that evening and suggested that we all go over to Follies. I had heard mixed reports but Alice assured us that it was a friendly venue - so off we went: Alice, Maria, Sharon and her partner, Samantha and myself.

When we got there, we looked around and apart from the cabaret, could only see one other tv in there. We certainly got our fair share of glances - but they were friendly enough so we got on with enjoying the shows and the dancing.

At one point I was dragged (if you'll excuse the expression) down onto the dance floor by a girl who didn't believe that I had a daughter who is older than her! Mind you I think she was only after my fur jacket - which she proudly put on! (No more Columbo remarks from Lisa!)

Monday 28th April Sue, one of the girls I've been chatting to at Michelle's, lives not far from me in Manchester and I'd invited her round to the flat for a drink.

She duly arrived with a bottle of wine and we settled down for a chat. This was the first time she had ever met another tv - and seemed fascinated by some of the incidents I related from my 30 odd years of dressing. (At least she didn't yawn with boredom!)

This wasn't the first time I'd met another TV who had never been out - and I'm always happy to try to help such girls get over their natural apprehension at going out and meeting other TVs - especially of going into a group without the faintest idea of what to expect. That, after all, was the driving force behind my web site.

Seeing them finally come to terms with being tv and getting out an enjoying the companionship (and having fun) rather than sitting at home feeling guilty gives me immense satisfaction!

May 1997

Tuesday 6th May Barbara and her husband Dave are two friends I made when I was previously working near Manchester. Barbara says she sees Helen just as another of her girlfriends! Unfortunately, they can't get down to the Village as often as they might like - so while chatting to Barbara on the phone one evening she suggested that I go round to her place for a coffee one evening as Dave was working nights that week. This was the night.

I'd been there a few minutes when her phone rang - it was her sister Jean, who was going to call round. Jean was aware that Barbara had a number of tv friends that she meets in Paddy's - but she had only previously met a TS called Catrina.

When Jean arrived, the three of us were soon chatting away quite naturally which I found fabulous. Hopefully, Jean will be encouraged to visit Paddy's in the very near future. Barbara told me later that Jean had been very complimentary about me - and had said that she thought I looked like Elizabeth Taylor - I guess that's a compliment (for Liz of course *g*)!

Friday 9th - Sunday 11th May

This weekend promised to be hectic.

I had a long-standing arrangement to meet up with Karen from Scotland and a friend of hers, Suzie, to show them around the Village on the Saturday evening. Karen had just joined Vanity Club UK that week - so it was a double pleasure to introduce her to the scene (especially as it was to be her first time out in public).

I had also arranged to help another tv get a complete outfit together. Liz was due to come and stay at the flat on the Friday to give us the evening to chat about what she would need and the Saturday to go shopping.

But, best laid plans of mice and men (not to mention girls) etc......

On Friday, I had a call from Liz to say she wouldn't get down Friday evening but would be over early Sat morning. OK. That posed problems trying to fit in all she needed to get - but I could draw up contingency plans.

Then Karen phone. She was in a motel just outside Manchester, but Suzie hadn't been able to come with her. I suggested that Karen come straight round for a coffee; which she did. We stayed up chatting 'til about 1.30. Before she left, we had arranged that she would come round to the flat the next morning and join Liz and myself shopping.

Saturday

Liz had promised to be there early. I tried her mobile phone at about 8; no answer. Karen arrived and we kept waiting for Liz - and trying her number. No joy.

At 10 I decided I had to cancel the contingency plans made for Liz as she had clearly been delayed somewhere and we had no idea when, or even if, she would appear. Karen and I headed into town. After making some totally unnecessary (in my case) purchases, we got back to the flat at about 12.30 to find several messages on the answer machine from Liz - the last announcing that she was heading for Blackpool for a walk on the beach. I called the mobile number - but there was no reply.

Then she finally called again and turned round to head back to us.

We had a serious time problem if Liz was to be outfitted ready to go out that evening. Fortunately, we found that some of my clothes would fit and were suitable. But we still needed to sort out a wig, undies, shoes and, if at all possible, make up.

Time was against us - especially as Liz has a bad back which can flare up and disable her so rushing around really wasn't a possibility.

We managed to sort out a wig and undies and had almost completed the selection of a pair of shoes when the mobile phone went again. Another business emergency demanding her immediate attention meant curtailing the shopping expedition and the planned evening out.

Liz dropped Karen and me back at my flat then, after a cuppa (cup of tea), she left.

Karen and I then got ready to go out. While Karen had a bath, I prepared a quick snack for us - which, in Karen's case was virtually untouched. Her excuse was that she was just too excited to eat!

The village was quite quiet that evening - probably the time of month when people look at bank balances and time left before the next pay cheque and decide that there is too much month left at the end of the money and stay home! But there were still a fair number of girls out around the Village.

From Paddy's Goose, we wandered around to the Via Fosse where we met up with another TV called Sandy and a friend of hers (Jason?) who is also TV but wasn't dressed that evening having only recently moved to Manchester and had not had time to get sorted out. The four of us had a drink in the VF then went over to Follies Galore - which is rapidly becoming one of my favourite venues in spite of the fact that it charges TVs admission which most places in the village don't.

Nevertheless, a visit to Manchester really isn't complete without going to Napoleons - so we walked back there - Karen making them point that the mere fact of being able to walk around was a fantastic feeling in itself.

There were a lot of the regulars (including Jacqui) in Naps and Karen was, I hope, soon made to feel at home. She certainly met a lot of girls that evening - many of whom complimented her on her looks and refused to believe that it was her first time out dressed

Well done, Karen!

Karen gives her own view of the trip on her home pages Karen's pages which seems to suggest that she enjoyed herself!

Tuesday 27th May

It's been quite a week or so!

Several of my outgoing e-mails seem to have been going astray - and attempts to co-ordinate a Vanity Club UK trip to Stoke on Trent have been severely hampered to say the least.

Fortunately, I seem to have worked round the problem!

But if you wrote to me recently and failed to get a reply - do re-send your message. I reply to all messages I receive which ask questions (other than those asking for dates - sorry guys but I'm not interested).

I get quite a few e-mails from visitors to my pages - and I welcome, really welcome, them! Many are from other "girls" thanking me for putting into words what they've felt and for showing them that they are not alone. I always, always, reply to such messages and to those left on my guest book (providing an e-mail address is provided, of course). I frequently get replies expressing amazement that I have bothered to reply. Sometimes these are very touching.

One arrived last week from a TG in Texas, who, as far as I can make out, has never previously had any contact with other TGs. Her loneliness cried out from the screen as I read how she had wept when she opened my message! "If I ever found time to write again" she asked "would I please address her by her femme name". I replied that no TG with access to the internet is truly alone. We only have to log on to Michelle's/Donna's or TG Forum or one of the other chat lines and we soon make friends from all round the world.

Her next message said that she had been working her way through a pile of serious academic messages when she suddenly found herself being addressed as Martha! The surprise of this made her cry again!

It's moment like that that bring a lump to my throat - and more than justify the time spent developing my pages.

I'm not sure if I mention elsewhere - but this story reminded me of a friend at one of the groups who was given an ultimatum: "Stop dressing or I leave and take the children and you will never see them again".

Stopping dressing permanently simply isn't an option for a transvestite. We can try; we may even suppress our need for a while. But it is part of us and ultimately will not be denied. Any attempt to do so almost invariably leads to other problems.

I believe my friend recognised this.

She knew she could not stop dressing - but could not face the future without ever seeing her children again.

She took the only way out of the dilemma that she could see.

Her death solved nothing.

Perhaps if she had had access to friends on the internet she could have talked through the problem; perhaps she would not have done so because she certainly had several friends she could have telephoned.

We will never know.

But I do know that if my pages can help other TGs to come to terms with being transgendered; or make them feel better about themselves - and if this prevents just one single pointless suicide - then that's sufficient justification for my pages.

I'll never know if this is the case.

I do know that I have helped a few girls to come out and meet others - and I get a real kick out of seeing their obvious pleasure. And that is its own reward!

One of these girls is Sue.

You've read about her earlier. On Saturday 25th May I got back from work to find a message on my answer machine. Was I around that weekend? Could we meet up.

I tried to call her back - but the line was busy; probably on the internet - maybe at Michelle's; no not there. I decided to deal with my e-mails then tried Michelle's again. Sue was on the line. We chatted and I persuaded her to come down to the village that evening albeit not dressed en femme. We arranged to meet up in Paddy's Goose and for her to come round to my flat the following evening.

There had been a football international that day in Manchester - and the city centre was busy - even Paddy's Goose had its share of visitors. When I arrived there was a group of strangers occupying our usual "Tranny Corner". As I went to the bar one of them said hello; when I responded, an incredulous look appeared on one or two faces. Perhaps they hadn't expected my voice to be quite as deep! One of them seemed befuddled by drink and seemed to have a problem trying to reconcile my looks with my voice - then the penny dropped and he realised what he was looking at!

The group left as I was being served and I heard one say "of all the (expletive) bars to choose".

At least we got our corner back!

Sue arrived soon afterwards - and a number of my friends came and went during the evening - and Sue had a chance to chat with goodness knows how many other people; many of them TGs of all sorts.

The bar closed at 11pm - leaving us 20 minutes "drinking up time" before the staff really started to plead with us to empty our glasses. A crowd of us made our way over to Follies Galore.

I keep saying it - but this and Paddy's Goose are now my firm favourite venues in the Village. There is a good mixed crowd; a superb TV DJ (whose name is I believe Lucy) - she never stops! (Unlike most that you see who make a few bored remarks (if you are lucky) about the next record - then slouch back until it's finished) Lucy is fantastic - her jokes are risqué but stop just short of being offensive and really crude and you rarely see her without a smile on her face! She also performs in many of the short cabaret acts - which are professional enough to be on any club stage anywhere — indeed; the whole show would not be out of place as a main feature in a Las Vegas hotel. I kid you not. The place is great! I also love the mix of music played. So many clubs think they can take the top ten, re-mix them, switch on the amplifier and turn it to maximum and that's it! Not at Follies! You get a total mix from 1920-1997. It's certainly my sort of variety and judging from the rest of the audience, it's theirs too. Even teenagers who weren't around when a lot of the music was being covered by other artists 15 years after the original hits seem to love them!

But even though I love Follies, no evening in the Village would be complete for a newcomer without a visit to Napoleons so, eventually, we headed there!

In Naps, we met up with an old friend of mine, G, from Didcot. Seeing her in Napoleons threw me completely and although the face was familiar, I couldn't place her. I felt so terrible! Especially when she reminded me that I used to give her a lift home from the Oxford group while I was working down there! All I can say is that we do tend to associate people with certain environments and had I seen G in Oxford or the Way Out club - the brain would have made the link; but 200 miles away it didn't. Oh G - please excuse me! Put it down to senile dementia!

G was with an RG called Vicki who has her own page on the web. I've e-mailed her and we may well be meeting up on Wednesday night at Northern Concord.

Sunday 26th May Sue came round in the evening bringing a bottle of wine and a small present as a thank you for me having run her home the night before (or, more accurately, earlier than morning). Now Sue is tall 6'4", but slim - and when she gets her look together with an appropriate wig she is going to turn a lot of heads believe me!

Once she had changed into a blouse and skirt, we sat and chatted and she told me that she had been awake at 5am that morning reliving every conversation she had had the previous evening! She said that she knew I had told her that she would fit in and that everyone was friendly - but until she experienced it for herself, she couldn't appreciate just how easily she would fit in.

The next step is for her to come out dressed! Won't be too long I suspect.

Monday 26th May A couple of weeks ago I went round to Barbara's, an RG friend of mine, for a drink and her sister Jean popped in and we had chatted 'til gone midnight.

For those of you with the attention span of a goldfish, Barbara is an RG married to Dave - both regulars in Paddy's Goose ('though not as frequently as they would like). As far as Barbara is concerned, I am just one of her "girlfriends".

I've been offering Barbara and Dave a meal ever since I moved back up to Manchester - but never seemed to be able to tie them down as Dave often works nights. So, having met Jean I told Barbara that if Dave couldn't make it, she should bring Jean instead. Tonight was the night!

"Don't do anything special" I was told. "That Haddock Pie you did for Faye sounds nice". OK - so it's an old family standby - or my interpretation of it! It's actually dead simple: poach some smoked haddock in milk with onion until the fish is tender and flaky; drain the milk into another container through a sieve; put the haddock and onions into a dish; cover with slices of tomato (or tomaito if you're from USA - hi Patty!); using the milk you saved earlier, make a cheese sauce (packet is fine) and pour over the haddock & tomato; cover with mashed potato (I add a good dollop of butter and grated cheese when mashing the potato); garnish with more sliced tomato and add grated cheese to the top and pop into a hot oven for about 15 minutes. Voila! Helen's Haddock Heaven!

OK main course taken care of - and I'd bought a variety of cheeses to finish with. Easy Peasy! There was a bottle of wine in the fridge - but needed something more to start with I thought. Harvey Wallbangers - that will do nicely; I'll make a jug of them! First buy a jug (well I've not long been here); Oh, and some tumblers too!

Now what was the recipe? 6 measures of Galliano, 6 of vodka and one of orange juice? No that doesn't sound right! Oh yes - one measure each of Galliano and vodka and 6 of orange juice!

Now my jug holds six tumblers - so six measures of Galliano; six of vodka hmmm! The jug already looks about 1/3rd full. Oh well! Fill up with orange juice - quick taste. WOW! Right; the table is laid; the lounge is reasonably tidy; fresh flowers in a couple of vases (vaises to you Patty). Better get myself ready! Off with my apron, skirt & blouse - run a nice scented bubble bath and soak for 20 minutes; then into the bedroom to dress and make up. While the moisturiser soaked in, I popped onto the internet to check my e-mails and deal with any urgent messages.

Then back into the bedroom to apply the rest of my make-up. I absolutely HAD to look my best tonight!

A glance in the hall mirror as I left the bedroom - well, I'll never be a contender for Miss World - but I was satisfied that I'd done the best I could. Just my nails to put on now. I decided to do them in the kitchen so that I could watch out for Barbara & Jean. I was just applying the last nail when I saw them arrive. Perfect timing.

Having taken their coats, and accepted a pot plant and bottle of wine that Barbara had kindly brought, I poured them the Harvey Wallbangers - adding a slice of orange and a cocktail cherry!

The meal would be ready in about 10 minutes so we relaxed and enjoyed our drinks - Barbara complimenting me on my flat and the way I'd decorated it. I gave them both a quick guided tour - not that there is much to see!

"You have got serious problems if your wife comes to visit" she warned. "This is not a man's flat! You would have to get rid of all the little knickknacks - and the dressing table". As that was precisely the effect I'd been aiming for when doing the flat, I was delighted!

Dinner was ready so I fetched the dishes and put them on the table - inviting them to help themselves.

As both of them had at least two helpings of the dish, I think they enjoyed it! There was certainly nothing left at the end.

We made ourselves comfortable on the couch and easy chair and proceeded to just chat for the rest of the evening; finishing off the wine Barbara had brought and the rest of the Harvey Wallbangers!

I can't describe how great it felt to just be regarded as another girl by Barbara and Jean; everything seemed so natural and totally relaxed. They really are a terrific pair of ladies! I look forward to more "girls" nights with them!

Friday 30th May The Club, Stoke on Trent, had a "birthday party" featuring Toyah Wilcox and Sarah, one of our members from Birmingham, had suggested that this would be an ideal opportunity for a Vanity Club UK get together. Who were we to argue?

As well as members of VC UK and their wives/ friends, I had organised a group from Manchester who also wanted to go. Up to Friday, there had been 10 of us planning to make the trip - but, at the last minute, 4 dropped out. The rest of us: Sal (RG) and Martin, Jacqui, Kath, Caroline (RG) and I met up in Paddy's Goose. We then headed south down the M6 motorway to Stoke. It's about 40 miles.

Apart from being home of Ruby's Club, Stoke is world famous for pottery (the area is called the Potteries); for soccer fans - it also produced Sir Stanley Matthews and Gordon Banks; it was the birthplace of Mitchell - designer of the Spitfire and of the captain of the Titanic and there are links to Alcock of Alcock and Brown aviation pioneers! One or two other people have also been born there - including me! In fact, my whole family come from the area - and whilst they wouldn't recognise me, when dressed, I do resemble my mother as she was 25 years ago so that could just make people wonder - perhaps mistaking me for my sister! Oh well!

Now I may have been born in Stoke, but I've only spent a few months at a time there and, in any case, they keep changing the road systems in the city centre; but I had a fair idea of roughly where the club was and knew I could get within 100 yards or so - then it would be a case of working our way through the one-way system and back roads to get to the door.

In the end it was easier than anticipated and we were soon inside Ruby's Pub, located above the Club.

I saw some faces I recognised from the VC UK pages and introduced myself to Sarah and Stacey - and met their wives Anne and Karen. Not long afterwards, Jayne and Samantha arrived - with another group including Deborah (with whom I had chatted many times at Donna's Den). I also met up with a couple of local girls who are members of NC. So, it was a real mixture of making new friends and greeting old ones!

We eventually made our way downstairs to The Club itself; it was heaving and seemed as though it couldn't take any more people. Not so, by the time the cabaret started, there must have been a 50% increase! Toyah was brilliant and so was Ruby. They looked as though they did a double act all the time - it was so well timed.

Penny, one of the girls, had managed to obtain some VIP passes for a private party after the show and a few of us went upstairs. Unfortunately, this meant that I had to leave my own guests in the main bar. I stayed upstairs for an hour or so hoping to meet Topyah and Ruby - all the time conscious of Sal and Martin waiting downstairs. Ruby did eventually arrive and having had a brief chat with her I decided I really could not leave Sal and Martin waiting any longer and went back down to them.

We then left the club and headed back for Manchester (Jacqui, Caroline and Kath having departed some time before).

It was an excellent night. The Club is a brilliant venue and if Sarah suggests more VC UK get togethers there, she will certainly have my support.

What's next? Well, May certainly seems to have been busy and enjoyable. Hopefully June will be equally interesting. Friday 20th/ Saturday 21st June sees another VC UK get together in Blackpool.

In the meantime, no doubt I shall be out and around the Village.

Sunday 1st June.

I had a phone call this evening from Samantha who is on a course in Leeds this week. She is planning to go over to Blackpool tomorrow night to see Lynda who runs the guest house which I've stayed at a few times. "Which way are you going" I asked. The obvious route would take Sam not far from my flat! We agreed to meet up at a service area on the M61 north of Manchester and go on in one car from there.

This would be a good opportunity to check out arrangements for the forthcoming VC UK gathering.

In fact there would be several other friends at Lynda's that evening - Stephanie; Trixie and another Linda.

Monday 2nd June.

We made it in no time - although, if air traffic control had had us on radar, I suspect Sam would have lost her pilot's license for low flying under the bridges!

Hugs were exchanged all round together with the usual mutual insults as we were admitted to Lynda's!

Sam and I hadn't changed before going to Blackpool - so we had a coffee and then headed for our bedrooms to get transformed ready for a visit to the Flying Handbag.

Some hours later; it was back to Lynda's - six of us in one car; with Trixie, Linda and me on the back seat and Lynda lying across our laps; keeping her head well down as we pulled up behind a police van!

A cup of coffee and a few sandwiches; then it was time for Sam to get changed again - she could hardly go back to the hotel dressed! Then it was back into the wingless jet; ignore air traffic control again and head back towards Bolton and my car; then on to Leeds for Sam while I drove more sedately back to Manchester.

Tuesday 3rd June PC Disasters! I switched on my PC and found it refused to load Windows 95 other than in safe mode - which did not give me access to the internet! It kept coming up with error messages. In DOS mode it also refused to recognise the CD drive.

Microsoft suggested trying to replace the registry file - which I did. Without success. If that failed, I had been told, you will need to re-install Windows 95! Then reinstall your applications! The thought did not appeal!

But I was left with no option! I couldn't use the CD drive so had to use floppy disks for Win 95! It still didn't work afterwards.

Wednesday 4th June Sue had told me that she planned to be at NC that week - her first time out dressed! We met up at Blooms and had a chat. She looked great! But felt reluctant to go out in daylight as she had decided to go for a striking look with her own hair rather than use a wig.

As I had arranged to meet Sam again in Paddy's Goose; I reluctantly had to leave Sue - hoping she would join us later when the light faded.

There was some of the usual crowd in Paddy's when I arrived. Then Faye, Jackie (RG+) Penny and Julie arrived from Leeds; followed, not too much later, by Sam.

We joined an RG, Myra, who was waiting for a coach to Ireland from the bus station opposite. Myra was lamenting the fact that her partner, who is TS, had left her. She asked where else we were planning to visit and if we minded if she joined us.

We then wandered around the corner to Dotz and listened to the live music for a while.

Sam and I then accompanied Myra back to the coach station for her bus - then rejoined the others, and all of us moved on to Follies Galore.

To say it was quiet is an understatement.

I've said it before, and I make no apology for repeating it, this venue leaves everywhere else in the village standing. IF YOU ARE IN MANCHESTER - GO THERE. Ok, I KNOW there are more recognised TG venues in the Village and that this is the wrong side of the road. I know, too, that everyone goes to Naps because everyone goes to Naps (so if you want to see friends, you need to be there) but there is absolutely no comparison in terms of venue, music or DJ. This is no criticism of Naps - just that Follies is the best venue in the area!

Sam decided that she wanted to call in at Naps - so she left before me. I caught up with her after staying for a couple more floor shows; by which time she was ready to come back to my flat to change before returning to Leeds.

Thursday 5th June/ Friday 6th June More attempts to sort out the PC; eventually persuaded it to run Windows 95; but all the links to the applications had been lost - and the CD drive still refused to work.

I was, however, able to get back on the net! I sent an e-mail to a friend who I thought might be able to help sort out my sick pc.

I also had a chance to chat with Deborah who was planning to visit me that weekend and go round the clubs. She confirmed that she was still coming over on Saturday afternoon.

Saturday 7th June

Went out to my car to go to work for a few hours to find a vacant space where I had left it! Returned to the flat and phoned the police. The car had been involved in a pursuit and abandoned after hitting something. It was, however, driveable. I was given the name of the garage where it had been taken. I called them and said I would come over to collect it. "You can't drive it" I was told, "it's too badly damaged" They made it sound like a total loss!

I called my insurance company who said they would arrange for an engineer to inspect it but, as it sounded like a total loss, they could not offer me a courtesy car. At a minimum, getting any decision from them would be bound to take at least a week and probably cost me £150-200 to hire a car for that period. I considered my options and decided I had to have transport. I had already been toying with the idea of cycling to and from work. So, I decided to visit some used car lots and, after about a six-mile walk, ended up at a second-hand cycle shop - where I bought a bike - which at least meant I could get to work on Monday. By the time I had ridden the 5 miles back to the flat I was sweaty and feeling decidedly unfeminine.

Debbie eventually arrived; we had a quick chat over a cup of tea; then got changed and headed down to the village in her car.

As usual, our first port of call was to be Paddy's Goose. As we walked up the road, in broad daylight, with other people around, Debbie remarked that it felt fantastic just walking around as we were! This was only her second time out in public (other than at a support group) - the previous trip having been to The Club in Stoke (mentioned earlier in my diary). That had been in the dark and had been amongst gays/ TGs so was not at all threatening - apart from some lesbians in the toilets suggesting that Debbie should be using the gents! They had been slapped down by Sal - who is only about 5ft tall!

Now here she was, in broad daylight, in the centre of a major city, walking down a road!

In Paddy's Goose, we met up with Catrina, Fiona, Sal (renewing their acquaintance from Stoke) Pam, and more of my friends during the course of the next few hours.

Pam, Debbie and I then went over to Follies - pointing out other Village venues as we walked from one end to the other.

Follies was a lot busier than it had been on the Wednesday - but there are rumours that it may close in a few weeks! I certainly hope they are false.

In spite of the fact that there were very few TGs in the predominantly straight clientele, Debbie and I eventually made our way down onto the dance floor and were soon "bopping" the evening away. Debbie was struck by a dress a real girl was wearing and told her that it was fabulous and asked if she minded Debbie asking where she had got it. The RG was flattered and pleased to tell Debbie it was from C&A! "I can't believe I did that" Debbie said when we eventually left Follies. "Actually, asking a girl where she bought a dress so I could get one the same!"

We walked back through the village to Napoleons; the cool breeze blowing around our legs. Fabulous! I pointed out to Debbie that we had been virtually the only TGs in Follies apart from the DJ - yet she had felt totally relaxed.

In Napoleons, we met Jacqui and Kath whom Debbie had also met at Stoke plus a number of my other friends. Debbie was soon chatting and feeling totally at home.

I'd booked a taxi for 2.15 and it was eventually time for us to go out and wait for it.

Even just standing outside, waiting, was a thrill for Debbie!

Our cab finally arrived - I gave the driver our destination. He was quite pleasant and made some remark about not knowing what fares he would pick up in the village - but certainly hadn't expected two TGs! In fact I am so used to being dressed that it hadn't occurred to me that he might find it a bit unusual!

As we drove down one street, the driver pulled out to pass a bus he thought had stopped to pick up passengers to find that it was at the back of a long queue at traffic lights. Instead of pulling back in, he accelerated along the queue, cutting around the lights after they had turned to red; round another corner, then a third. I asked him if he had been one of the stunt drivers in Bullit! "No", he replied, "The Italian Job!"

I believed him!!

Miraculously we arrived back at my flat in one piece!

Debbie and I chatted for another hour or so until we decided we really ought to get to bed - Debbie on my couch, me in my bed (just in case anyone wondered!).

Sunday 8th June

The original plan had been to go down to the village in Debbie's car and leave it there overnight. Then use my car to go down in the morning and collect it. I had told Debbie that her car would probably be as safe in the Village as outside my flat! (I guess I was proved right!) This way, we would both be able to have a few drinks during the evening.

As my car had been stolen Friday night, we had to call for a taxi to take us back to Debbie's car- which had survived the night parked outside New York New York.

We returned to my flat via a quick shopping trip to Sainsbury's for some food.

We had hardly been in the flat for a few minutes when Jacqui telephoned; "Why didn't you call me to take you into town?" she asked. "If you need a lift checking out cars today - give me a call"

After Debbie left, I made some phone calls to find a replacement car and arranged to go and see one - a thirteen-year-old Astra. I took up Jacqui's offer of a lift and she came round to pick me up.

I inspected the car and decided it was a bit of a banger - but that the engine and mechanicals seemed reasonably sound. It was not a car I would normally wish to own or drive - but this was precisely what I needed for Manchester! I pointed out some of the defects I had identified to the seller and having negotiated a price of £200 for it, went to a cash point and withdrew the necessary funds.

Jacqui followed me back to my flat and stayed for the rest of the afternoon and joined me for tea. While she was there, the police from Salford telephoned about my Cavalier. The officer told me that they had spotted the car and would have had had no reason to suspect anything if it hadn't immediately sped off! They gave chase in a Transit van but, hardly surprisingly, could not keep it in sight. They then found it abandoned, the thieves having run off.

The officer sounded surprised that the garage had told me that the car was badly damaged - he said the damage was to the passenger door and the steering lock - but that he had driven it himself to the police station. If his assessment is correct, it seems possible that the car is repairable rather than a total loss. Which means I could end up with two cars in Manchester!

If that turns out to be the case, I might look at the possibility of using the Astra for short trips in town and find somewhere more secure to park the Cavalier for longer trips. This seems a bit wasteful. However, I much prefer the Cavalier but recognise that it is an attractive target for thieves. If I can get cheap third-party fire and theft insurance for the Astra it might still be a sensible option rather than sell either car. I shall have to await and see what the insurance company says.

I said earlier in my diary that May had been interesting. June has certainly started off with some "excitement" - but I can well do without this sort of problem!

Well, the insurance company seems to writing off the car. So, the "problem" of having 2 doesn't exist.

Wed 11th June

A friend of mine came over and fixed my PC for me - he described it as a bag of nails! We ended up in Follies Galore - where I was able to show Lucy the review of the club on my Havens page. Rumours of closure were, thankfully, false!

Friday 13th June

I was showing Jacqui the internet on my pc when it crashed again! I've been unable to sort it out (I suspect a virus or hardware problem)- so this update is being done in a Cyber Cafe.

Saturday 14th June

Sam & Jayne came up to Manchester & stayed at the flat. As usual we hit the town. As we walked into Follies Galore, Lucy said "Hi Helen, visited your home page & signed your guest book". With a personal invitation from the star of the show - how can anyone doubt that we are welcome here? As usual the show was brilliant!

Sunday 15th June

Had a phone call from Niki who I met in Blackpool saying she would be in M/c on Wednesday & could we meet up. She is now going to be staying at the flat - gives me another new girl to introduce to Follies! (I really ought to get a discount on the drinks there!) Or a retainer as their PRO (In fact I am actually qualified in Public Relations) As it happens, I had a phone call from Nikki on Wed evening to say she couldn't make it.

Friday 20th June

Off to Blackpool for a Vanity Club UK gathering!

Jacqui & Thelma are coming round about 6, then we are off to collect Sal (RG) before heading for the 45-mile motorway trip to the coast. Two cars for 4 off us? Well, we are trannies and it's not so much the girls who need the space as the luggage!

Sal is ready to go when we get to her house - just one small bag! Thelma said she needed petrol before we get onto the motorway (that's gas and freeway for overseas visitors) but we find ourselves on the motorway ring road around Manchester before we can stop for her to fill up. It's rush hour and the road are a solid jam. Takes us 45 minutes to go about 8 miles. Finally, we clear the ring road and head north-west for Blackpool; Thelma starts falling well back from me - so I slow down; still no sign of her as we approach a service area. Assuming that she will stop here for petrol, I pulled off. Sure enough, she pulls into the services and darts into the toilets - I thought she needed to fill up, not empty herself! Nerves apparently at the prospect of running out of petrol!

Back on our way! I had arranged to call Stacey and pick her and her wife up from their hotel and take them round to Lynda's for the BBQ planned for the evening (mind you, as it was raining, (so unusual for the Manchester area), there wasn't much prospect of a BBQ outside). But we were running a lot later than I had expected - so I increased my speed to about 70 (there could be police officers reading this page) to get there as quickly as possible.

Probably not a good idea bearing in mind the age and condition of the car; as we approached the Blackpool end of the motorway, the oil warning light started to flicker on and off. This had been my first longish trip in this car and I suspected that the oil or water must have become low.

Well as long as the warning light continued to go out, I figured there must be some lubrication getting through so decided to continue as we only had another 5 miles or so. The car got us to Lynda's guest house and we were soon greeting my friends from VC UK - plus the residents - Trixie, Linda (another one) and Mike. We were the last to arrive of those staying at Lynda's - in fact Sal and I were in the overflow accommodation - The Lancaster a couple of doors away.

The BBQ was well under way - so we joined in; it really isn't the same eating it indoors though!

Sal and I then went to our hotel and checked into our rooms and I got changed for the evening's planned visits to the Flying Handbag and Flamingos. I had phoned Stacey - and had arranged for them to meet us at the FH.

We all had a great time at both venues - and finally piled into a couple of taxis for the trip back to the hotel. Then stayed up chatting 'til at least 3am. We girls can talk about anything and nothing!

Next morning, I checked over the car and decided that the problem had been caused by a shortage of water - and maybe a lack of oil although it was still just on the minimum level; I topped both up and left it at that.

Then it was back into the hotel to change into something more appropriate for a femme weekend. Albeit toned well down as we were planning some shopping in town.

Thelma had disappeared on her own, Sal took herself off to the pleasure beach as she wanted to buy some seafood; Lisa, Sam (en femme) and Jayne decided that they would use Sam's car to head for the Cowbar for lunch and Jacqui and I (both en femme) accompanied by Karen and Suzie (en drab) decided we would walk into town and meet up with them later. Well we would have met up with them if we hadn't called in at a Superdrug for me to get some more makeup, the market for some tights (pantyhose) and visited so many dress shops!

I found a fabulous outfit in a second-hand store - it's middle eastern in style with a long top over baggy trousers; the top alone would serve as a dress. I tried to negotiate a lower price - but my heart wasn't in it and I paid the asking price of £22.

We eventually made it to the Cowbar to find that the others had left 10 minutes before. Well, we had taken more than three hours to get there!

In need of refreshment, we had a quick drink then started to make our way back.

Unfortunately, our route took us past a shop where Jacqui had seen a gorgeous green dress with a heart shaped cut out on the back surrounded by sequins and pearls; she had been very tempted to buy it on our way to the Cowbar - but had resisted the temptation. I tried hard to stop her going in; but lost the battle. She still wasn't able to negotiate a lower price for the dress - but I offered to lend her the money if she wanted to get it. She decided to try it on while I went to find a cash point. I returned to find Jacqui disheartened; the dress just didn't hang well at the front and she decided against it.

We eventually got out of the shop and finally made it back to Lynda's with only a few more purchases (for which I was as guilty as Jacqui).

A quick cup of coffee and it was time to go and get changed for the evening.

The others had arranged to come round to the Lancaster at about 8 for a drink before the taxis arrived to take us to Autumn Leaves restaurant.

The outfit I'd bought got a number of compliments and I was delighted. My friends Faye and Julie had come over for the evening but were planning to travel back to Leeds the same night. I pointed out that there was bed space in my room for them to stay overnight if they wanted to and they took up the offer.

When we got to Autumn Leaves, we had been given a long table right in the centre of the restaurant with other customers, mainly couples, on either side of us. I'm sure they didn't know what to make of us when we first arrived - but by the end of the evening they had accepted us without any embarrassment and seemed to enjoy our presence! Well, they could have paid a fair bit to get into Funny Girls to see such a collection of TG beauties!

The meal was absolutely superb! I can heartily recommend Autumn Leaves for anyone - dressed or straight. It worked out to less than £20 a head including wine.

After Autumn Leaves, we walked round the corner and some of us, at Jacqui's suggestion, went into Pepys' - we didn't stay long as it was a bit macho for my taste. We ended up in Lucy's bar just down the road.

I said earlier that I'd thought the top of my outfit would serve as a dress on its own (in spite of mid-thigh high slits up the side); it did!

Eventually we decided we had better get some taxis before the straight night-club discharged its crowd - so we reluctantly left Lucy's.

It had been a fabulous evening.

Sunday morning (just),

Sal and I went round to Lynda's; we had missed breakfast at the Lancaster - but Lynda soon prepared some for us. Several of the girls had already left for home - including Lisa, Karen and Suzie.

It was soon time for us to head back to Manchester too; especially as I was a little apprehensive about my car. In fact, I had decided not to travel en femme just in case it broke down.

As it happens, it gave no trouble. Whether it had been the low water level - or driving back slower or not having had to sit in a traffic jam for 45 minutes before getting on our way as we had had to do on Friday, I don't know. But it behaved itself.

Back in the flat that evening, I had a phone call from Stephanie, another of the VC UK girls who had been unable to make Blackpool. She was going to be in Manchester the next evening; was I doing anything?

Well, you just CAN'T let another girl down, can you?

Monday 23rd June

Steph and I met up in Paddy's Goose; had a drink in there - then went round to Via Fosse where we had a quick meal before going over to Follies Galore. As usual during the week, it was not exactly thriving - but that didn't bother me at all. Lucy still gave her best for those who WERE in and Steph and I had a lovely evening.

I had told Steph that I just had to leave the Village before midnight. Fat chance. It was gone 12.30 before we left Follies - then Steph wanted to call in Naps. So, we went in. And stayed 'til nearly 2. Not a good idea when you have work the next day.

BLACK TUESDAY (24th June)

Dreadful news today. I had an e-mail from Lucy saying that Follies had closed after last night's show.

I couldn't honestly say that I was surprised. It had been poorly supported during the week; even on a Wednesday evening when most of the girls were out. But the Village is a much poorer place without it.

BLACK WEDNESDAY (25th) More bad news.

Blooms Hotel is being sold and the groups using the downstairs bar have been told they must find alternative accommodation immediately. This includes Northern Concord. This means that NC has to find a new home and goodness knows how long that will take.

Ironic isn't it? If Follies hadn't closed, it might have been possible to make it the home for NC early in the evening on a Wednesday; that in itself might have encouraged more girls to use the venue.

That's life, I guess.

Great News

Well life is nothing if not unpredictable! Follies has re-opened at weekends - you can guess how I feel about that!

Sunday 29th June

I got back from one of my infrequent trips home to Cambridgeshire to find a message from Steph; she was back in Manchester on Monday; was I around?

Monday 30th June

It wasn't just Steph who was in town but Nicki as well. Nicki lives not far from my Cambridgeshire home and we had met before in Cambridge. The three of us got together in Via Fosse; then went round to Dotz. Piano bar and the New Union before ending up in Napoleons.

It had been a hectic month! What else does next month hold I wonder? Come back soon and find out!

Tuesday 1st July

Sue - a friend of mine who lives a few miles away - but whom I'd first met courtesy of Donna's Chat Line, came round for coffee this evening - as did Jacqui who also lives near me. (There are rather a lot of us in Manchester as you might gather).

Wednesday 2nd July Northern Concord might be virtually homeless at present but the girls still head for the Village on a Wednesday evening. In fact, I've heard that NC IS still meeting on a week-by-week basis at Blooms - but never know until almost the last moment if they will be allowed to use the premises.

Thursday 3rd July

I must be slipping. I didn't go out - or have anyone round to see me!

Friday 4th July

That's more like it - another excuse to go down the Village. Not that I need much encouragement! But you have to admit, the visit of a friend you haven't seen for ages is a reasonable excuse, isn't it? What do you mean you don't consider 48 hours "ages"? Well, Ok so I had seen Julie on the Wednesday - and Jacqui on Tuesday - but it must have been almost a week since I'd seen Kath!

Anyway, I was celebrating Independence Day!

Saturday 5th July

I was in Paddy's Goose with a bunch of friends when another TV came in and sat down at a table by herself - I told Jacqui to invite her to join us. She introduced herself as Brenda and when she told me that she was from Warrington I realised we'd e-mailed each other quite a few times - then Brenda realised that we had in fact met before!

On leaving Paddy's, we walked round to Dotz - then, surprise, surprise, ended up in Follies Galore. Don't worry I'm not going to bore you by going on and on and on about how brilliant Follies is. I will say that I had spread the word around on Wed evening that it would be open and was delighted to see a fair number of girls in there when we arrived - and particularly pleased when a couple of them came over and told me that they agreed that it was a brilliant venue (their words not mine - but who am I to argue).

Sunday 6th July

I'd been corresponding with a TV called Donna who had visited my page and e-mailed me as a result. As she lived in Manchester (I know, yet another one) I invited her and her wife Lynn round for coffee this evening.

Donna had come, as I'd suggested, in male mode - but with a change of outfit. (It was broad daylight when they arrived). While she went into my bedroom to change, Lynn and I had a chat over a cup of coffee. Donna finally emerged - not entirely happy with her makeup - but still looking as good as a number of TVs around the village who have been going out dressed for years.

Donna had brought a bottle of bubbly (the real thing) to celebrate her release from the closet - and to toast one of those rare and lovely creatures - a genuinely supportive and understanding wife - here's to you Lynn, you are fabulous!

The evening passed all too quickly but I promised to go over to their place next time when Donna gets back from an overseas trip in about three weeks.

Rest of July

The end of July brought another down; Follies Gallore has closed once more - although there is a possibility of it re-opening. Time will tell. Dotz is becoming much busier - especially at weekends with a reasonable mix of music compared with most venues around the village.

Some Saturday evenings there are queues to get into the New Union, Via Fosse and other venues - and most of the others that I visit seem to be busy. Is the need to cross Princess Street such a barrier? Perhaps so!

Well, I've spouted off about Follies quite enough; regular readers will know that I love that venue and consider Lucy to be the best DJ I've ever watched. I wish her well whatever happens. And she has my heartfelt thanks for all the great evenings I and my friends have spent in Follies.

But it's not been all doom and gloom.

Odyssey - the new venue for Northern Concord appears to be attracting back some of the members who were deterred from going to Blooms by the fact that it, too, was just outside the main part of the Village. Well, I DO understand that some of the girls are nervous about where they go and I can sympathise with them.

There was a letter issued by NC having a dig at some members who no longer go and those who just use the club to get changed and go out around the village. It was pointed out that newcomers need the more experienced members for advice - and that the cost of renting Odyssey depends on a reasonable amount taken over the bar. Fair comments - and I certainly agree that it's not reasonable for members to just use the facilities to get changed. Although they do point out that they pay their annual subs and the £2 admission charge - so why shouldn't they just use the club as they do? There are always two sides to every issue.

In my case, I often arrange to meet newcomers at NC, have a drink, then take the newbies off around the village. I don't consider this unreasonable. By doing this, I am continuing to support the group through my annual subs, weekly admission fees and paying at the bar; I'm supporting the aims of the group by encouraging others to join - and by taking newbies "under my wings" and showing them the village. I also support the group in other ways - writing for Cross Talk and maintaining the NC notice board on my pages. So, I'm fairly confident that I'm not the target of the criticism.

I agree wholeheartedly with Jenny and Mary about the members who think that they have outgrown the group and no longer need it - but exploit the facilities without putting anything back into it.

I've had a couple of other newcomers round at my flat recently: Theresa and Alison. Brenda also came to stay the night a couple of Fridays ago. In Alison's case, she was unable to change and come out on the town; but Theresa and Brenda both did. It was Theresa's first trip out - and she was very nervous to start; after visiting NC, then moving on to Paddy's Goose, she soon relaxed and had a great evening.

Brenda is far from a newbie - and has an excellent site linked from my list of friends.

On the last Sunday in July, I had a photosession at my flat for some wigs that Lisa - and I are going to sell from a joint "virtual shop" we are setting up. We won't claim to be the cheapest around - but our aim will be to develop a range of products which are of good quality at reasonable prices. In fact, I really should be working on getting that set up rather than on my diary! Lisa and I both, we believe, have a reputation within the T community of which we are proud - and we aim to keep those reputations by providing a fair service to our sisters.

The model for the photosession was a TS friend of mine Pam - she was really knocked out by the results of the shoot! Check out the pictures for yourselves!

After the session, Pam stayed on so that we could upload her revised pages for her site. (Unfortunately, Pam does not have access to the net from home at present). No doubt there will be another update soon to use the new pics!

Friday 1st - Sunday 3rd August

The first weekend in August was another Vanity Club UK gathering in Manchester. Turnout was a little disappointing, but Lisa came over as did Samantha and Karen.

In fact, I got back to my flat on the Friday to find Karen and Lisa parked outside. Samantha rang soon afterwards to say that it didn't look as though Jayne would be able to make it due to pressure of work - so she would be coming up on her own. Karen had been "booked in" at Jacqui's flat (which is just up the road from mine) - while Lisa and Sam were to stay with me.

We dropped Lisa's car up at Jacqui's flat at the same time as delivering Karen; Jacqui then brought us all back to my place where I made a spaghetti bolognaise (to help soak up the anticipated evening's intake of alcohol); soon after we had sat down to eat, Sam arrived - so I threw on a bit more spaghetti for her!

We were rather later than usual leaving the flat for the village and didn't get into Paddy's Goose until gone ten pm; hardly time to get in a couple of rounds before the bar closed; then it was on to Dotz followed by Napoleons.

We had arranged for a friend of mine who runs a taxi service to collect us from outside Dotz at 2am. We stumbled out of Naps just before the allotted time. Dotz is only a matter of yards away from Naps - but then, almost everywhere in the Village is only yards away from the other venues!

While waiting for Michelle (our taxi - no she doesn't drive dressed en femme) Sam approached a couple of GG's and invited them to chat; this led to us being invited back to Melody's place for a drink - which I have to say we declined (must have been mad). By that time, several other GGs had also joined us and we were all chatting away.

By 2.30 we were getting just a bit concerned about Michelle. But she eventually arrived having had a fair who hadn't known where she really needed to go!

So, it was back to the flat - and on with the coffee and a natter. We eventually stumbled into bed at about 4am.

Naturally enough, this meant that it was quite late by the time we got up the next morning - which didn't matter. Karen rang from Jacqui's and arranged to come down to us. After a good breakfast/ brunch, we decided to visit the "celebrated" Transformation - as none of the others had ever visited the Manchester branch (and, besides, Lisa and I needed to size up the opposition for out "Vanity Fair" venture.

Frankly, I admit that Transformation provides a service for trannies who are too timid to shop in normal shops; it's been the introduction to the tg world for hundreds if not thousands of girls. But they do charge very high prices for products - a set of boobs which appear to be identical to the ones I use were £375. I paid £120 (although they are now £140). Mine were bought from Bullen Healthcare a specialist surgical appliances company - which probably has a similar restricted market to Transformation in terms of customer base; I suspect Transformation probably sells more sets than Bullens - so probably enjoys better terms. The price being more than 2 and 1/2 times as much at

Transformation starts, therefore, to look a bit greedy (got to be careful what I say - don't want to find myself being sued).

It is accurate to say that very few regular trannies but anything from Transformation that they can get elsewhere. And almost everything they sell can be bought elsewhere if you know where to look.

Needless to say, we didn't buy anything from the shop - and headed off into the village for some lunch.

It was actually the first time I had ever been in Paddy's other than en femme! We enjoyed an excellent lunch; had a wander around the village in daylight; then called in at a department store to buy a few femme items en route back to the flat.

A quick nap was called for to prepare ourselves for the evening. I then made a few phone calls to check just who was going to be joining us for the meal that evening. I had originally booked for up to 20. Jayne and two others from Nottingham hadn't come; 4 from Blackpool had also dropped out; Suzie - who had hoped to come with Karen hadn't been able to make it; Jacqui herself was going to have to work and wouldn't make the meal. Sal and Martin weren't going to make it either - so 11 down! And the 5 spare places wouldn't be needed either. Then Jacqui rang - Angie wanted to join us; so did Julie from Stoke; Linda from the Lake district had left an entry in my guest book saying she was visiting Manchester with her partner Chris that evening - so I rang them and invited them to join us. Back up to 8. I phoned Metz and changed the reservation - making it for up to 10.

In the event, Angie decided she couldn't face it and dropped out - which meant Julie also failed to show. So, we were back down to 6.

But it was a good meal, albeit it short on service - and they added a service charge to the bill to cover the missing diners. Had they been open about this charge we wouldn't have complained - but just adding it to the bill made it look as though we had been overcharged.

After Metz we went round to Dotz.

I am not going to reveal what went on in Dotz that night - other than to say that Lisa fell in love with a GG across the room, went over to introduce herself and discovered that her name was Liza!

We met up with Jacqui and Julie in Napoleons. Plus, naturally, a lot of my other friends from the village. One lesbian friend looked across the room - "Who IS that girl over there?" she asked. "I fancy her, she's gorgeous". "Shall I introduce you?" I offered. "Do you know her?" she demanded "She is a REAL Girl isn't she; She IS isn't she?" As I called Karen over, I told Gilda that Karen was TV.

Gilda was astounded and told Karen that she was fabulous.

We tried to get into Via Fosse later - but the queue was too long; so, we decided to return to Napoleons. In fact, we didn't make it - we agreed we were tired of the constant pounding beat in Naps and decided to return to the flat as we noticed that Michelle was parked outside Dotz.

Jacqui, Karen and Julie joined us for coffee - and it was 5am before we broke up. I believe that Karen then effectively drove straight back to Scotland as she had a plumber coming that lunchtime.

Monday 4th

Barbara had invited me round to dinner - together with Dave, who is involved with Lisa and me in Vanity Fair. There would also be another Dave (Barbara's husband) and Jean, Barbara's sister. Barbara had helped us prepare the wigs for the photosession with Pam and we persuaded Pam to come with us.

Barbara had originally invited me around for a meal nearly two years earlier - but somehow a date had never been set. "I'm no cook" Barbara had warned. Well - she is. The meal was excellent and the company great! It was another fabulous evening.

Tuesday 5th

As I logged on to UKTV I saw that Ruth was on line. Ruth is an old friend of mine from Oxford - so I said hi; she asked if I knew Rosalind - and I said I'd only chatted briefly to her - the usual hi, how are you's when coming on line. As Ruth had also met Ros, she suggested setting up a private channel for a three-way chat. As we chatted, we found that Ros and I had lived in the same town and probably walked past each other in the street many times!

August 8 - 10

You will have seen above that while Lisa was up last weekend, she fell in love with Liza - and who can blame her?

Having chatted on the phone and been invited to call her again, Lisa decided she might come up to Manchester again this weekend probably coming up on her motorbike on the Saturday afternoon. Kath from Stoke was also due to come over on the Saturday.

Jacqui and I had already arranged for Kellie-Marie (KM) to stay with Jacqui for the weekend. I had a phone call when I got back to my flat after work on Friday to say that KM had duly arrived and was at Jacqui's - literally about 1/4 mile up the road from me.

"Errr, we have a problem" said Jacqui, "I've still not got any cooking facilities ...." (she'd only just moved into the flat and British Gas seem to be taking forever to arrange connection). "So, you want me to feed you " I said. We arranged for them to come down about 8 (which probably gave me 'til about 9 to prepare).

Fortunately, I'd just been to the supermarket - so my week's supply of salad and cold meats planned for 3 meals for one were quickly made into one meal for 3. The different cold meats planned for different evenings looking like I was offering a selection of cold cuts!

I'd also had a message from Ralph to say that he was in M/c that day and had Faye's PC with him. He arrived a short time later but couldn't stop long - and after we had checked that Faye's pc hadn't suffered in transit, he left again. I phone Faye and told her the news. She decided to come over and get it that evening and go down the village with us. The three meals for one - which had become one meal for three was now going to have to stretch to one meal for four. Just as well I tend to like a reasonable amount of meat with my salads usually.

Jacqui's 8 o'clock eventually became about 9 (as expected). After eating, Jacqui went off to fetch Angie and the rest of us headed for the village in Faye's small car. We parked and walked up the road. KM later remarked that she had expected to be stared at - and one of her main impressions of the evening was attracting no more than a glance just as any girl might receive. There she was, dressed en femme, out in public for the first time in her life, in the middle of one of the UK's biggest cities - and no-one was taking any notice!

Of course, for some girls such a lack of attention would be devastating!

It was actually a relatively quiet evening for the Village. But even so, KM probably met 20 or so other TGs - and saw quite a few others; we were also joined from time to time by other friends of mine who are regulars down the village. We sampled, I think, Paddy's Goose, Dotz and Napoleons.

Eventually we decided to call it a night and returned to my flat. Faye had already left for her drive back to Leeds as she had to work the next morning. As usual, we continued to chat over a coffee as KM started to come down from her high! We even went onto Donna's Den for a quick chat.

The next day, I had to work in the morning. When I got home having done some shopping en route to replenish the larder, I quickly checked my e-mails and no sooner had I disconnected than I had a call from Jacqui. "Is the coffee machine on" she asked. "Does it rain in Manchester?" I replied. "We're on our way down" she told me.

KM and Jacqui arrived at exactly the same time as Lisa pulled up on her motorbike. KM had also come over from NI on her bike - so spent some time looking over Lisa's impressive machine.

Lisa and I decided to eat out - and arranged to meet Jacqui, KM, Kath and Angie (another local girl) later in Paddy's Goose or Dotz.

We headed for Metz where we were offered a table outside next to the canal. As we walked over to the bar Lisa told me that someone seemed to recognise me; I turned round to see this guy sitting at a table waving - "It's me, Lucy - well Tony when dressed like this", he said. Lucy from Follies Gallore - the best venue in town when it's open. I introduced Lisa and asked Lucy whether there was any more news about Follies and was told that she was still involved in talks and that it certainly wasn't dead. "a lot of us are keeping our fingers crossed that Follies reopens" I told Lucy.

Lisa and then went over to the bar to order a drink while waiting for our table. A "straight" group then came up behind Lisa and we received a few glances - I remarked to one of the girls that Lisa and I were admiring her dress - she thanked us for the compliment and started to chat; her group then moved out of the bar just before we were told that our table had been cleared. By the time we walked out to it, the group we had just been talking to had taken it.

The waiter explained the situation to them and they gave up the table for us. We continued to chat to Joanne, the girl whose dress we had admired, we then ordered a meal which would guarantee that I would make no further progress that night in an attempt to slim down to a size which would look good in such a dress. Such is life.

We eventually made our way round to Paddy's Goose and met some other girls in there - but no sign of Jacqui, KM, Kath or Angie. So, after a couple of drinks, we walked round the corner to Dotz Piano Bar.

The others eventually arrived and we continued to chat and drink and listen to the music until we decided that we should visit Napoleons. Naps has always been a good venue for TGs and it's only right to repay their hospitality with at least a visit sometime during an evening in the village.

At about 2.30am we decided it was time to head home - well to my flat - where a large pot of coffee was soon made (I do find that many TGs, while they enjoy a drink, don't need alcohol to enjoy themselves - the dressing gives them enough of a buzz!). Having said that, I had imbibed a glass or two of wine during the evening - so my car was left in the village overnight and Kath gave Lisa, KM and myself a lift; while Jacqui took Angie back to her place - then joined us later.

Sunday morning, Lisa and I returned to the village to collect my car - then having packed, and loaded her bag on the bike, she headed back to the east coast.

Jacqui had to do a taxi service that evening for her ex-wife - so dropped KM down to my flat for the evening.

KM said that the trip had exceeded her dreams and would be back as soon as she could. She is one of the fortunate minority whose wives accept their transvestism - and had phoned Maggie several times during the weekend. It eventually transpired that Maggie had no problem with KM coming over to M/c for a weekend en femme - but wished she was able to come too. Next time Maggie!

It had been another memorable visit.

And another notch on the belt - as yet one more girl has been shown the fun side of being TG! KM joins Ruth, Sue, Karen, Deborah & Theresa who I've also helped to introduce to the pleasures of going out dressed (plus Suzie who came to a VC UK weekend in Blackpool with Karen). Donna, Alison, Angela - your times will come! I also look forward to introducing a lot more girls to the scene in Manchester - even if it's not their first time out! These include: Ruth, Paula, Laura and Rosalind from the UK; Alexa who I met with Lisa; and my friends from Donna's Den especially - (and no insult intended to any whose names I leave off) - Alex, Patty, Zoe, Cindy, Antoinette, AK from SA, Rene & Delores from Oz, Vera Emm, Marina, Rainbow Rhonda, DG, and about a dozen more girls I chat to regularly. Then there are my friends from UKTV on IRC, including Fran who hasn't been for so long she probably needs a refresher course on the place!

I gather that Samantha may be planning a trip up this way next weekend - and Lisa intends coming up again the following week. That's the Mardi Gras weekend in the village.

Well, this brings the diary back up to date. But come back soon - there will probably be more added next week

August 1997 Mardi Gras Weekend

August 21-25 Last weekend was the Mardi Gras in Manchester. This is the major festival to raise money for the Gay Village Charity. It means that the entire village would be packed out.

Lisa and Samantha had already planned to stay with me to attend at least part of the celebrations. Lisa was to arrive on the Friday afternoon - Sam on Saturday. My TS friend Faye from Leeds was also planning to come over; then I heard from Julie from Hull who was also looking for somewhere to crash out. Fortunately, Jacqui lives just up the road from me - so we had some overflow accommodation available.

I'd also invited Pam to get changed at my flat for the Saturday evening. Things were going to be hectic - but we would cope somehow.

As Lisa was in London on the Wednesday. she decided it was a bit insane to drive back into the wilds of East Anglia on Thursday then come across country to me on the Friday. It made much more sense to come straight up on the Thursday.

So, Thursday evening arrived and I returned to the flat to see Lisa's car parked outside; we soon got changed and headed down the village for a meal in Metz. As we waited for a table, a GG came up to me - it was the girl who had been the chef at the Blue Cafe - as the last I'd heard from her was that she was emigrating to New Zealand I was rather surprised to see her there.

I told Lisa that this was, in my opinion, the best chef in the world. Well, she is the best I've ever encountered. I still drool over the meal she had prepared at the Blue Cafe for New Year's Eve 1995.

It appears that her move to New Zealand had been postponed and she was now working at Metz. She had not, however, been responsible for any of that evening's fare. Nevertheless, the meal was very good. Nice surroundings, good food and pleasant company - what more can one ask?

We certainly were not planning a late night on the Thursday as I had to work the next day. But we still spent a relaxing evening in Dotz bar.

Friday - In the office, some of my colleagues were discussing Mardi Gras. It seemed at least one was planning to attend on the Sunday. As they have no idea about Helen, that could have led to problems - although the chances of bumping into them in the crowds were slim and that of them recognising me even slimmer.

Lisa and I had already booked a meal in Via Fosse as Metz's kitchens were closing for the Mardi Gras.

The Village was already getting set for the festivities; roads were closed and premises were decorated.

Lisa and I were a tad later than planned getting to the Village - can't quite recall why this should have been as I'd returned from work by 4pm and don't usually take 4 hours to get ready!

As we sat down for a meal, another girl approached us and asked if we minded if she joined us; she told us her name was Caroline. A few minutes later Molly arrived with her wife. They too, sat down at our table for a few minutes. Molly had still to change so they left us when the food arrived.

After the meal, Lisa and I wandered around to Dotz - with Caroline following - or so we thought - but somewhere in the hundred yards or so, she disappeared.

The usual crowd in Dotz was already being supplemented by visitors to Mardi Gras. Lisa, as usual, found an attractive young girl to have her photo taken with!

Quite a few of my friends came and went during the evening - many ending up, as we did, in Napoleons later.

Once again, we didn't stay out too long and eventually returned to my Astra to wend our way back to the flat. (The original intention had been to leave the car in the car park until the morning so that I could enjoy a glass of wine or 12 - but the car park had to be cleared by 6am for tents to be set up as part of Mardi Gras. There was no way I'd be up in time to collect the car at 6am! So, I'd limited myself to a couple of glasses of wine over dinner - and as that had been 5 hours or so earlier, I was well within the law).

Saturday morning - Lisa and I got up leisurely, had a late breakfast/ brunch while waiting for Sam to turn up. We then got changed and headed down to the Village in Sam's car.

Luckily, we were able to park on the edge of the area - just round the corner from Paddy's Goose. Paddy's is a typical British Pub, well, apart from the clientele, that is. It's a favourite with trannies - and there is nearly always a crowd of us in there on Wednesdays & Saturdays.

However, when Lisa and I had wandered round there on the previous evening, we'd found that they'd set up a sound system with a very large and extremely loud speaker pointing straight at trannie corner! It was simply not worth thinking about staying in there. If I'd been able to think!

We had done an immediate about turn and walked straight out again - telling Alan, the landlord, why we were not stopping.

By Saturday afternoon, the sound level had been reduced - still loud but not as loud. We decided to take our drinks outside in any case where a few tables had been set up continental style.

Oh; just realised, haven't said anything about how we were dressed.

Well. Sam was in her usual style - shortish dress showing a fair bit of leg. Lisa was in a pair of very tight and VERY short shorts. I'd decided that I could either dress right down as I would normally do for day time - or go over the top myself. I decided on the latter. Out came the ball gown I'd made for last New Year's Eve. Well one simply has to dress for the occasion!

Across the road from Paddy's was a mobile police station set up for the event. Lisa and Sam decided they wanted their pictures taken with a couple of constables. In the true spirit of Mardi Gras - the police obliged.

We then wandered around the place - having a drink or two in Dotz & Bar 38 (nice and air conditioned with a fabulous wash basin in the loo area). While we were in Dotz, Lynda, Linda, Trixie and some of their friends from Blackpool came in. As you will have read previously, these are good friends of ours and our hostesses for VC UK get togethers in that town.

Then back out to watch the end of the parade of floats.

We had arranged to pick Pam up from her flat at 6; so, we left the village just after 5.30. We were actually early getting to Pam's and I wasn't at all certain that she would have seen us. Pam is rightly cautious about getting known in her area - and three trannies sitting outside was not going to be discrete. Especially as we had been spotted by two separate groups of kids.

I told Sam to drive round the block again. By the time we returned, Pam was standing one the corner of the road and we soon had her on board.

Back at my flat, Faye and Julie were waiting for us.

We all trooped in and drinks were made/ served. Then we played musical mirrors (if you moved from the mirror - someone else took your place so you had to find another one).

Parking was going to be rather more of a problem this evening - so we decided to get a couple of cabs to take us down the village.

The streets themselves were absolutely heaving; Paddy's Goose was so crowded we didn't even try to get through the door - so we headed straight for Dotz. Ruth was already there - she doesn't get over to the village very often these days so it was good to see her again.

The evening passed with a confusion of meeting old friends and making new ones, chatting to girls out for their first time; persuading Anne to join VC UK and come to Blackpool with us next month (not that she needed any persuading); chatting to JulieZ about a mutual friend of ours - Paula; wandering around the street for a bit of fresh air, then back into Dotz or Naps; buying hot dogs; having one or two compliments - and one or two less complimentary remarks from drunken oafs. (They KNOW what the Mardi Gras is about - so why are they surprised to see trannies there?)

While I was in Napoleons, some guy came over to me and said "hi, I'm your neighbour from no 9! You drive the blue Astra, don't you" His lights had been on many times when I'd returned from the village - so he'd obviously seen me on several occasions. However, his tone suggested there was nothing to be concerned about - and, in any case, what was he doing in Naps? I didn't deny that I lived in the next entrance to the flats and after this briefest of exchanges he moved away again.

By about 1.30, Naps was absolutely packed out, it was like a sauna - and we had decided to get some air again for the nth time that evening.

By now the crowds in the streets were getting totally drunk - and both Lisa and I felt the time had come to call it a night. There wasn't any serious sign of trouble - but it would not have taken much for a fight to start and I, for one, did not fancy having to go to casualty with blood dripping onto my dress!

Kath's car wasn't too far away, so we gathered the clan together and asked who wanted to leave and who was staying. Faye, Sam and Julie decided to hang one for a while - "Just don't lock us out of the flat" asked Julie; "We'll be up chatting for an hour or so. Providing you're back by 3 you'll be OK" I told her.

As it happens, it was 4.30 by the time they got back. They had only stayed another 30 minutes they told us; but had then had serious problems getting a cab. They had even tried to walk out of the village to the main railway station (not a good idea). They'd had no more success there so had returned to the village.

I have to say that I had anticipated problems getting cabs - which is one of the reasons I'd suggested leaving when we did. I certainly wasn't in the best of moods by the time the strays returned - but we all make mistakes. I served Julie a drink she asked for with rather bad grace - then made it quite clear that I expected everyone to call it a night and let us get to bed. Kath, Pam and Faye were intending to stay up at Jacqui's; Lisa, Sam, Julie and I - at my flat. By the time that they got back, the bottle of brandy Lisa had brought with her on Thursday was empty.

Next morning, I was woken by the phone. It was Sam - who had left at 8am and was back home. At least she had rung to thank me for my hospitality - although a bit later in the day would have been more appreciated.

Faye arrived a few minutes later and chivvied Julie into getting up. They then left - while Lisa and I walked up to Jacqui's flat to collect Lisa's car from the secure compound up there. I'd expected Julie and Faye to go a different route - so hadn't bothered to ask them for a lift - but was amazed when they drove straight up the road past the block where Jacqui lives without having even offered us a lift.

All of my friends will be welcome to come again. But I certainly won't be leaving part of the group down the village again to come back later.

After the gang had left, I settled down to watch the Belgium Grand Prix. The race had only just started when the doorbell went - probably Jacqui, I thought. Come to collect her keys.

It wasn't. It was Brenda - well, at least it wasn't 10 am this time. We sat and watched the GP - after which she left to go down to see the Mardi Gras. Jacqui also turned up later to collect her keys.

Although Monday was a bank holiday, I decided to go into the office and do some work for a few hours. I then went back to the flat.

So, out of four possible days at Mardi Gras, I'd actually only spent Friday evening and Saturday down there. A waste? Possibly. But I don't feel the pressure to take advantage of every single opportunity to dress. I can, and do, dress every evening in the flat. I go out at least Wednesdays and Saturdays every week. It's not a matter of "having had enough" - or "being bored" simply that a GG wouldn't necessarily dress up every night and go out on the town. That's an interesting comment I've just made. Comparing my life style to that of a GG.

Certainly I spend as much time en-femme as I do in male mode. I would also prefer to spend even more time en femme. So, am I a potential full time TV/CD - or TS? At this stage, I'd say the former.

Well, the diary is back up to date again. I'm out again tomorrow evening; Deborah is coming up next weekend. Fran, who runs the NC website, is supposed to be bringing Donna and her wife Lyn to NC the following week, then it's VC UK in Blackpool the weekend of 5/6/7 Sept; Deborah is bringing another new girl out on 13th. So, plenty to do yet!

5th-7th September Vanity Club UK, Blackpool - a Windy Weekend

My grotty Astra car (automobile) has been leaking oil for some time now. So even just a 50-mile trip to Blackpool was not an attractive prospect in it. Fortunately, both Samantha and Lisa had offered to pick me up en route. As Sam would have Jayne with her and be in a smaller car than Lisa; it seemed sensible to take up Lisa's offer.

I arranged to take Friday pm off work - to give me a couple of hours to get back to the flat to pack - ready for Lisa to arrive at about 2.

Things were going according to plan. I'd returned to the flat via a cash dispenser and Sainsbury's supermarket (well, not quite according to plan, Sainsbury's had run out of my favourite make up remover wipes). I tried to call Lisa - but she was in an area where mobile reception was poor - so I had to wait until she called me back.

She had been delayed setting out and was running about 90 minutes late.

That was fine by me. It meant I had time for a bath and to get changed en-femme for the trip to Blackpool rather than travelling en drab.

As I finished my bath, I remembered a note that I had been left asking me to get in touch with the council's works department to arrange for them to repair the kitchen window frame. I phoned their office and tried to sort out a suitable day for them to do the work. Not easy when you work full time and only get paid for the hours you work. I eventually agreed to let them have a spare set of keys and that they could send someone straight round to collect them. I was still wearing my bathrobe when the bell went. I gave the bloke the keys then walked back into my kitchen. I glanced down at my feet and realised that I was wearing a pair of white mules which in no way could have been taken for male shoes!

I was getting made up when Lisa arrived; then the phone rang. It was Paula; an old friend of mine whose own plans for the weekend had been curtailed by events - but I'll leave her to tell you about that when she gets her own web site re-established. The consequences of this call were, however, that we were delayed by about 15 minutes in leaving. 15 minutes which probably proved to be critical later.

We finally got under way. The trip to Blackpool should be a 45 -50-minute drive.

Not this trip.

We had been en-route about half an hour when we came up to a queue of traffic stretching as far as we could see into the distance. We tuned in to a local radio station as they were reading out traffic report. No mention of the M61 on which we were stationary. So, either the cause of the problem had only just occurred - or it was of insufficient importance to warrant a mention. There was, as we later realised, a third option. That we were outside the area covered by that station. You can guess which it was can't you?

We sat there for 20 minutes without any appreciable progress.

We searched the channels to find another local station - and tuned into another traffic report advising "avoid the M61 northbound at all costs!" A hay lorry had caught fire and the motorway was closed! Not much consolation when you are sitting in the jam! It was well over an hour later before we had crawled along to the junction where traffic was being diverted off the motorway; and another half an hour before we were able to resume our journey at anything approaching a reasonable speed.

Those of you who have followed the reports of VC UK weekends on both my site and Lisa's may recall that Lisa reported having been disturbed by a noise emanating from my own nether regions when we shared a bed in my flat (nothing else - just the bed). (OK to put it clearly, I had farted.) This news was published on one of the most widely read sites in the UK.

Well, you may have noticed that the sub heading for this report is "windy weekend". A reference which is not restricted to the weather I can assure you.

Since Lisa's report on my solitary release of surplus gases, Lisa has been a regular visitor. Let me tell you that her comment about that single occasion really was a case of the pot calling the kettle black.

As we left the M55 and headed in to Blackpool, Lisa happened to comment that she had not had problems with wind that day.

Then it happened.

There was a loud noise which could have been mistaken for a balloon being released was it not for the accompanying aroma.

I have rarely been assaulted by such a smell since a holiday job on a farm which included having to clear out the pig sty!

We opened the windows of the Jaguar to clear the air - and it was only the fear of losing my wig which prevented me from sticking my head out of the car for the remainder of the journey.

Later I was talking to another of the VC UK members in the dining room when there was a general exodus from the lounge - accompanied by screams of "LISA". A sheepish president of the VC UK came into the dining room!

Well, that's probably my tenure as VP of VC UK over!

So, what else did we get up to in Blackpool. The weekend was, of course, affected by Diana's funeral on the Saturday.

Lisa and I had finally arrived at about 6.45 - 2 ½ hours after setting out from my flat on what should have been a 45-minute drive.

After greeting the others, and having a drink and a chance to recover from the trip, we change ready to go out for the evening. Previously in Blackpool, we had tended to visit Flying Handbag and Flamingos on the Friday and Lucy's on the Saturday. The previous visit, we had harangued by Deana - the DJ from Basils - for not having been in there to see her. She had claimed to be the hardest working TV DJ in the country. Regular visitors to my pages will know that I am a great fan of Lucy who used to be the DJ at Follies Galore. IF Deana was better than Lucy - then it would be an act worth seeing.

We decided therefore to see just how Deana did compare.

Maybe Deana will claim that Di's funeral affected her performance. But, in my view, there is simply no comparison. Sorry Deana. This is not a criticism of you; simply the fact that Lucy is in a class of her own. But, then, Basils is still going and Follies isn't - so the fact that I preferred Follies and Lucy to Basils and Deana isn't much of a basis to get a general consensus. (Mind you, if you could understand what the DJ was saying in most of these venues, it might help - why oh why don't they keep the volume to a level where the output isn't distorted? Or install sound systems that are clearer or maybe, just speak more clearly?) After Basils, we made our way round to Lucy's.

On a Saturday, it's virtually impossible to move in here. Friday was still busy - but you could, at least, get to the bar.

As usual, we got chatting to other visitors and enjoyed a very pleasant evening.

On the Saturday, almost all of the UK was closed until 2pm "as a mark of respect for Diana - Princess of Wales funeral".

I didn't even bother getting out of bed 'til gone 10 and, as usual when away, dressed en femme before having a late breakfast.

Lisa, Karen, Samantha, Jayne and I left Linda's for a walk in to Blackpool to find a pub for a drink. We got to the Cow Bar just after two to find it was still closed - but with a sign saying it would be opening about then - so we waited.

After a lunch (yes, I know I'd had breakfast not long before) and a few drinks we headed back to Lynda's. We did a bit of shopping on the way. By now it was really quite chilly with a strong wind which kept lifting my skirt and threatening to remove my wig. There were also some heavy showers.

That evening we had a superb meal at Autumn Leaves before moving on to Flamingos - getting to the club at about midnight. While having a drink in the bar on the top floor, I saw a group of girls wearing T-shirts which all had a comment about "googlies" on the back. Being nosy, I went over and asked them what it was all about. Turned out they were a ladies cricket team (a "googlie" for overseas readers is a type of delivery when bowling the ball). I had an interesting chat with Anne, one of the members. She explained that they were having an end of season trip - and had to observe Ten Commandments for the whole evening one of which was that they could not "wimp out" and leave before the club closed!

It was, she said, the first time she had ever spoken to a trannie! Come to think of it, it was the first time I'd ever chatted to a member of a ladies cricket team (at least knowingly).

Later that evening Anne came over and asked if I'd do her a favour. She had broken one of the Ten Commandments earlier and had to pay a forfeit specified by the others. In this case it was to give me a kiss. "Would I mind". Even as a lady I'm a gentleman - so I obliged - and gave her an extra one for good measure :-)

As with all weekends at Lynda's, the time passed too quickly and, as Lisa had a 6-hour trip back home ahead of her, we left soon after 11 - taking just 45 minutes for the return trip.

OK Diary updated again.

This week looks like being very hectic.

Monday Steph and Hazel are coming over; Tuesday, I'm helping Lynda and Michael from Blackpool to buy a PC; Wednesday is NC night - with another newbie due; Thursday I'll probably work late to get information prepared for a regular Friday am meeting; Friday evening I have just realised that I have a clash of dates. Paula asked if she could come up when she rang on Friday as I was getting ready to go out. I had quite overlooked an arrangement to go round to Anne and take some photographs of her with Pam. Saturday Deborah and Michelle are due up to join Paula and me.

See how things work out.

October 1997

I'm conscious that there has been a significant gap since my last diary entry. It's not that I haven't done anything - just that I've been too busy to write it up.

To those girls who have visited and introduced themselves to me; I'm sorry not to have given you a mention on these pages. For some reason some of you seem to think that this is an accolade - can't think why.

I was chatting on UKTV on IRC when a "Kym" appeared for the first time; she asked where I was from and told me she was in Manchester. I responded with "Manchester *grin*". We soon established that we lived about 3 miles apart. Kym had been out dressed - but not for a few years. The next evening, I received an e-mail addressed to Pam (I act as a PO Box for them while she is off-line) from Kym; I sent an acknowledgement and told Kym I would pass on her e-mail to Pam that week. Kym and I were both on channel again on the Sunday. After a few minutes, she asked if she could come round and see me for a face-to-face chat. I asked when she could come and she said "20 minutes"; "make it 30" I told her. We met again on UKTV on Monday and Tuesday - and I encouraged her to come along to Northern Concord on the Wednesday. She asked if I could give her a lift - so I agreed to do so.

There were a number of other UKTV chat girls coming to NC that week - including Adele. I had helped Adele to re-draft an announcement to her company's clients that she was transitioning. She was coming down to Manchester for a few days - and I had invited her to dinner on the Tuesday. We had a good old natter that evening before she took a taxi back to her hotel.

One of the subjects we discussed was a posting that I had sent to TGFolk-UK forum concerning what makes the difference between TV and TG - and what causes either condition - and where I saw myself in the spectrum. This had been sparked off by some comments from Adele and another TS friend of mine, Toni, earlier - in which they had said what they had felt prior to recognising that they were TS and not TV; to a very great extent, it seemed to me that I shared almost all of their conditions. This had led me to reconsider my own position and express concern that I COULD at some stage come to the same conclusion as they had. That posting and the reactions to it form the basis of a new page I have been working on. I look forward to getting other people's reactions to my views.

We also discussed the possibility of organising at TGFOLK-UK forum gathering in Manchester. An idea which is now going to become a reality on 5th-7th December. Theresa from the forum has suggested that we could also use it as an occasion to honour some of the girls who work so hard for the TG community and provide so much support. I can certainly think of several who deserve such recognition. It would be great to organise a national event along these lines - not just limited to the internet.

On Wednesday, I had Julie staying with me so that she could also go to NC, the two of us then went to collect Kym - whose mother came out of their front door with her to say hello. (What a fortunate girl to have an understanding mum!). At NC, I gave Pam the e-mail from Kym and waited for her to read it. "Are you going to respond to that one Pam?" I asked. "Yes, I think I should" she replied. I then stood aside and introduced Kym to her!

I had made a sign for UKTV and set it up on a table so that other girls from the chat could find us. We had Heather, Helen Jane, Toni, Kym, Adele and Kelly (I do hope I haven't overlooked anyone!). From NC, we moved on to Dotz. I was dropping Kym home so we left relatively early while some of the others went on to Napoleons.

On Thursday, I met Adele again in Paddy's Goose and the two of us visited Via Fosse and Dotz again. The following weekend, we had arranged a gathering of some of the VC UK girls in Manchester. This started by Karen and Suzie wanting to visit Manchester and suggesting that we notify all of the other VC UK girls. Julie had also decided to join us; Suzie then dropped out but both Karen and Julie had invited other friends from the net to join us - they could only make it for the Saturday night. Sounds confusing? It's not finished yet. I'd also had an e-mail from an American girl (Monique) who was going to be in Manchester that weekend, she in turn had made contact with another UK girl - Mandy.

Monique had also contacted Molly - a friend of mine. Molly had booked a room at Rembrandt on the Saturday; Monique and Mandy were staying at New Union. Molly and I had decided that it would be a good idea to have a meal together on the Saturday night.

She and I have had debates over which is the best venue in the village for eating! I used to support the Blue Cafe; she favoured Via Fosse. Unfortunately, the Blue Cafe closed months ago - so I booked dinner at Metz (couldn't possibly be seen to be backing down to Molly's preference *grin* (in fact we had discussed it and both agreed on Metz)). With Karen due at about 5.30, and wanting to make contact with Monique, I had a fair bit to do on Friday afternoon after work. Fortunately, we finish at 3.30pm. So, I dashed round to the local Sainsbury's, got in food and other supplies for the weekend, then dashed back to the flat.

As I was locking up my car, a familiar face appeared - Alison who had been to see me some weeks earlier and with whom I'd corresponded. She had come out to her wife and they were trying to come to terms with their situation. "I was in Salford and popped over on the off chance" she said. Conscious that I had planned to tidy the flat before the others arrived - and get other chores done, I realised that these were going to be deferred. There was also a message from Faye saying she'd like to join us on the Saturday evening.

Alison and I had a bit of a natter. I really don't know that I was able to contribute very much - but maybe just talking about her situation helps her to clarify her own thoughts - and get it off her chest. I left a message for Monique at New Union; Karen arrived; Alison left and Karen and I got ready to hit the village. There had been no response from Monique and when I called New Union again, I was told that she had gone out - but she knew that we would be in Paddy's Goose so we left it at that. Karen and I met up with a number of the other girls in Paddy's Goose and left messages for Monique should she turn up. Jacqui from just up the road was travelling back overnight with Thelma - (who lives in the same tower block as Jacqui) after Thelma's "op".

Karen and I had got to bed by about 3am. We were woken up at 8.30 by Jacqui calling to say that they had arrived back safely - thanks Jacqui! End of plans for a long lie in to prepare for Saturday night! Jacqui asked if the coffee pot was on - so I said no, but it soon would be. I'll be down in an hour then, she told us.

Later that morning, Karen went to collect Tanya from the station; the three of us then popped out to drop their things off at Jacqui's and do some shopping - including a card and present for Sal - whose birthday it was. Julie arrived soon after we returned; Tanya and Karen went up to Jacqui's (where they were staying for the night); Julie went to the station to pick up Vikki - and I started to get ready by diving into a relaxing bath! GIRL - did I need it!!! Vikki's train had been delayed so it was 6.45 before Julie and Vikki returned to my flat. By then, I was virtually ready to go out.

I called Jacqui and asked how the other two were doing (she was going to be joining us later). "Nearly ready", I was told. "OK - I'll collect them then rather than getting a taxi." I told Jacqui; "Just give three rings on the phone as you are leaving the flat and I'll send them down;" Jacqui had said. Just after 8, we pulled up outside Jacqui's block. No sign of the other two. 10 minutes went by. 15. Then I saw Karen walking out of the entrance. "Jacqui decided Tanya needed some beard cover" Karen informed us. 20 25 30 minutes after arriving, I sent Karen back in to find out what was happening. "If she isn't ready in 2 minutes, she'll have to take a taxi." I told her. Karen disappeared.

Another 10 minutes went by. I had done a circle so that we could check the entrance to the block again - and, if they hadn't been in sight, I was going to be leaving them as we had other girls waiting for us in the Village. As it happens, they were just emerging. It was 8.45 before we left Jacqui's block. We were at Paddy's Goose 10 minutes later. I went over to greet the others - and introduce myself to Monique (who had made contact that pm). I gave Pam her usual batch of e-mails, said my hellos - then said "hang on while I get a drink, I need one" Sal and Martin came into PG as we were about to leave for Metz. Everyone joined in a chorus of "Happy Birthday" - and I gave Sal the card and a small gift.

Unfortunately, we could not stay much later as our table was booked for 9.30 - so Faye, Molly, Monique, Pam, Karen, Julie, Tanya, Vikki, Jane, Mandy, and I all trooped round to Metz. As I was returning to my seat having taken some pics of the group for Monique, I bumped into Lisa - one of the chefs at Metz. Lisa had been the chef at the Blue Cafe - and, in my opinion, the best I've ever known. I asked for her recommendations for the evening's meal and she suggested the lamb or the tuna. I chose the lamb - and it was superb; as were the Lyonnaise potatoes I had with it. Molly had to concede that Metz was (almost) as good as Via Fosse and that we might now have to agree on our recommendation for eating out in the Village.

I DID point out that the former chef from Blue Cafe was now working at Metz. We agreed that the ambience in Metz was almost as good as in Via Fosse - and that the food was better and the prices a bit lower. As the setting had been a significant disadvantage that Blue Cafe had had over Via Fosse - but their chef was now working in Metz - we agreed it was "honours even". Unfortunately, Faye's meat (not the lamb) was burned on one side and some of her new potatoes were not cooked. Other than this, everyone else's meal was excellent. After Metz, we went round to Dotz - but it was so crowded that we decided to go straight into Napoleons. Molly, Monique, Mandy and I later had a wander around to Via Fosse for some fresh air, then popped into Dotz. We eventually returned to Naps where we met up again with Sal and Martin. Pam and a couple of the others had left (even Jacqui had disappeared) by just after 2am - but I invited Monique, Mandy, Sal and Martin and, of course, Karen and Tanya back to my flat.

With nine of us it was rather a squeeze but we had a few more drinks plus some snacks and chatted until Sal fell asleep on the carpet and Tanya was looking totally shattered. A taxi was called and Karen and Tanya decided to walk up the road to Jacqui's.

As it was 4.30am, the pubs would have been closed for hours and very few people would still be around, I didn't consider this to be any risk for them. Monique, Mandy, Sal and Martin shared a taxi. I unplugged the telephone from its socket and, having sorted out bedding for Vikki and Julie, went to bed myself. Sunday, it was lunchtime before we returned to the village to collect my car. I returned to sort out the disaster area that had been my flat. Kym came round again a bit later to choose a new wig from my catalogues.

I had had an invitation to a 60th birthday party for Wally at Dotz. Jacqui and I had provisionally arranged that I would pick her up about 8 and that I would only stay about an hour before heading home for an early night. Kym stayed longer than anticipated and it was already past 8 before I could think about redoing my make-up and changing out of a casual dress into something more suitable for the village. I decided that by the time I had got changed, picked Jacqui up and driven down to Dotz, it would be well past 9. I wanted to be in bed by 10.30 latest which would mean leaving Dotz again after just half an hour.

So, I decided to cry off. Instead, Jacqui came round for a coffee and Kath picked her up from my place. It's been a hectic couple of weeks. The next highlight is likely to be the end of the month when Paula is due to come up. She is bringing Mary from Swansea with her. Then it's Vanity Club UK in Blackpool in November. and the TGFOLK-UK forum gathering in December. Watch out for the reports.

November 1997

What a start to the month! I had Paula coming to see me for the weekend and bringing Mary - who I had chatted to many times on the net - either at Donna's Den or on UKTV on IRC. This was to be Mary's first time out and Paula's first time other than a support group. Molly had also asked if there was a spare bed (or floor space) available. Then Adele had asked if she could also stop over. That, unfortunately would have stretched things a bit too much. Fortunately, I have some wonderful friends, including Jacqui from up the road from me, who are happy to help out with spare beds.

Paula and Mary were planning to come up fairly early on the Friday and had arranged to meet Sue (another regular from Donna's Den Chat) in Paddy's Goose. I was to join them when I finished work. Molly had spent Wednesday night at my flat and was going to be returning to Manchester at about 5pm on the Friday; Adele was flying down from Aberdeen on the Saturday and would need collecting from the airport about lunchtime. I had been looking forward to this visit more than most because of the problems that Paula had been through over the past year. She and I had exchanged dozens of e-mails and phone calls over the past year. As you'll see from my friend's links, she is my adopted "daughter"! This is no comment on the other girls I've had to stay with me - but I had been extremely concerned about Paula and I knew that the fact that she was coming up to Manchester really meant that she was getting over some of her problems.

By 3.30pm on Friday, I was ready to leave work (we finish early on Fridays). By 3.50 I was walking into Paddy's Goose; there was no sign of the others and I assumed that they had not expected me to get there quite that early and had gone to do some shopping. I was, of course, not en-femme at this stage and nor would the others be dressed when we met. This was only the second time that I had ever been in Paddy's en-drab. Not that this stopped the staff recognising me!

The others arrived just after 4. I saw them walking past the window and wondered if they would recognise me. I'd met both Sue and Paula before when they were en drab so I was at an advantage. I waved to them as they came in - when I asked if they would have recognised me, I was told yes - from your smile! What an incredible compliment! Molly had also said that it was my smile/grin that had given me away on the Wednesday evening when I'd stopped to pick her up as she walked to my flat. I have to say that I am absolutely delighted if my most noticeable feature is a smile!

We had a quick drink with Sue before leaving to meet Molly at the flat. Unfortunately, Sue was unable to come out with us over the weekend due to domestic difficulties. We had an e-mail from her over the weekend saying how much she envied us.

By the time we returned to the flat, Molly had arrived and was waiting for us; we went in and I made the introductions. After a chat, it was time to start getting ready for the evening. I phoned Jacqui to see if she could lend Paula a set of bra-fillers as she had not been able to get any before the weekend. Jacqui called a mutual friend and arrangements were made for them to be brought down to the village later; in the meantime, Paula had to make do. Kym came round to meet the others during the afternoon and we asked if she was coming out that evening. "Probably not" she told us.

As Paula was unable to drink due to medication, she offered to drive us in rather than take a cab. Our first port of call was Paddy's Goose (again). We had a few drinks in there. We had been in there for about 20 minutes when I noticed Paula (I think it was) look up with a smile on her face as she looked at someone behind me. I turned round to see Kym about to grab me from behind! I was not at all surprised to see her - in spite of her saying she doubted if she would be out. Kym had been in male mode when she'd called round earlier but was now en femme. Let me tell you - she is gorgeous! No, I don't "fancy" her - just as Paula is my TG daughter, I regard Kym as a niece and take an aunt's pride in a lovely girl in the "family"! We then made our way around to Via Fosse for another drink before strolling down to Metz to book a table for the Saturday evening. At first, they said they were fully booked - but managed to make space for us. It's great when you are treated as a VIP! :-)

We then wandered around to Dotz piano bar where we stayed until it was time to go into Napoleons. Walking around the village is one of the things that new girls find so incredible. We walk past dozens of other people who just accept us - maybe smile pleasantly or say hi. We do occasionally get small groups of straights who make less polite comments - but these incidents are rare. Having said that, we did encounter one such group as we went round to Dotz that evening. They made some comment about us being men - I responded with a comment that the others found amusing. Trouble is I've forgotten what it was! No doubt Paula, Mary, Molly or Kym will remind me. I don't usually bother replying to such comments and I'm not sure why I did that evening. (See anecdote "More of")

Dotz was its usual welcoming venue - as indeed are most in the village. I organised membership cards for Paula and Mary (Molly, Kym and I were already members).

Napoleon's was relatively quiet - which was nice as it gave the others a chance to get used to the venue without being overwhelmed. There were other girls in there of course and, as it was Halloween, they were serving a free punch. Goodness knows how many glasses we had between us. Angie arrived with another newcomer - Lisa. She had brought the bra fillers for Paula. We eventually called it a night at about 2am and returned to the flat where we sat and chatted for another hour or so.

On Saturday morning, we got up earlier than intended - about 8.30. After a lazyish breakfast, we headed into Manchester to do some shopping. Molly had identified a fancy-dress shop which sold cover all make up - so we parked near Paddy's Goose and walked into the city centre. We found the shop "Anything Theatrical" 53 Tib St. where the owner was very helpful. I realised that they had distributed their leaflets at Northern Concord so felt quite comfortable discussing make up with him. Molly and I both made our purchases. We all then headed for Boots (a large drug store for those outside UK) where I restocked some powder and blusher and Molly bought some nails. Paula then wanted some ear studs - so we went into the Arndale shopping centre (the target of an IRA bomb a couple of years ago); I also found some nice earrings for the evening. By now it was time to make our way back to Paddy's Goose where we were hoping to meet up again with Sue.

We ordered lunch in PG and, as we were eating, Sue arrived. I'm quite certain that she was jealous (in the nicest way) of our Friday evening. We were only sorry that she could not have been with us. It was amusing for me in PG to be ignored by several regulars who would have said hello to "Helen". I had to leave at 12.50 to get to the airport to collect Adele - so I left the others to their own devices.

Adele's flight was on time so I just had to wait for her to collect her baggage. She also recognised me as she emerged from the gate (I'm not sure whether I should be pleased or worried about this!). Adele was excited because she had sent out a letter to her clients announcing that she was transitioning and the reaction to this had been positive so far. As I had helped to write the letter, I was also over the moon about the apparent success rate! I told Adele that the copy-writing fee was a bottle of champagne at dinner to celebrate!

It would have taken about 25 minutes to drive back to my flat from the airport - but we called at a supermarket en route. The others arrived soon after we returned to the flat. Adele was to stay at Jacqui's flat which is at the other end of the road from mine (about 200 yards) - so, after a chat, Mary and I walked up there with her. On our way back out, we met Thelma who also lives in the same tower block as Jacqui. Thelma has just had GRS - and it had been Jacqui who had looked after her while in hospital and afterwards. (I have such wonderful, thoughtful, friends).

Mary, Paula, Molly and I had decided to get into the village early so that we could visit as many places as we could. So, by just before 7, we were ready to go. As arranged, we rang Jacqui and told her that we were on our way to collect Adele. First stop, of course, had to be Paddy's Goose. We were far earlier than usual and none of the other girls were out when we arrived. Kym joined us shortly after we got there. The six of us then walked around to Churchill's - which was remodelled earlier in the year. I had not been back since - but it really is a lovely place now. There is a sort of "library" area upstairs - and there are plenty of tables downstairs for meals. I really shall have to try it for a meal sometime.

Although I live in Manchester, I had not visited a number of the venues that are on Molly's recommended list - I'm quite happy to learn from anyone - so it was Molly's tour for the first part of the evening. We visited Velvet, Prague and Bar 38 as well as Churchill's. While I took the girls into Bar 38, Molly popped back to PG to see if Pam was in there and they then joined us.

We didn't have time to visit any more venues before dinner so we made our way to Metz. The Maître d' saw us as we walked in and indicated that he was just preparing our table; he then waved us over. Adele ordered her bottle of Champagne and we all drank her health and wished her good luck. The meal was excellent - Molly had very kindly insisted on paying for me as thanks for allowing her to sleep on the floor in the flat. However, Paula wanted to pay for us all - and a battle started when others tried to make contributions. I'm not at all certain what the outcome was. It was a very generous move by Paula - thank you!!!! Thanks too Molly!

Goodness knows what time it was when we left Metz for Dotz. I think we were all past caring! All tranny evenings in the village simply have to end in Napoleons - and ours was no different. The usual girls and, equally usual, there were several new girls out. (Not including my crowd). I got chatting to a couple of girls from Dublin and Warrington who asked if I was the Helen from the web! Such notoriety! :-)

I noticed that Adele and Kym were having quite serious conversations. They are both TS - Kym had just arranged a first appointment with Russel Reid for the end of the month and I could guess what the conversation was about. I'd also realised that Kym had been a bit down earlier. I heard Adele mention getting together with Kym on Sunday and suggested that the two of them should come round to my flat for dinner - so that they could have a good chat. They took up my offer.

I left them to it and re-joined the others. We danced and chatted and drank. Chatted, drank and danced; drank, danced and chatted. Gradually my remaining energy started to fade. I could see the others were reaching the same point - so we decided to call it a night. We didn't even stay up chatting much that night and were in bed by 3.

Sunday

We got up fairly leisurely - Paula, who is a computer service engineer, had agreed to upgrade my PC and use the parts we were removing plus some new ones to build a replacement machine for my daughter.

This went reasonably well apart from not, initially, being able to get Windows to use the high-resolution settings. Thanks, Paula, for doing the work and Ralph and Kym for the parts involved. There is one problem having upgraded my "bag of nails" as Ralph once called it to a halfway decent P166 with 32Mb Ram, Trio S64 graphics card and 2Gb & 1.2Gb hard drives. Unfortunately, at the office, I'm stuck with a 486-50. The comparison between the two is now even worse. I shall have to start putting pressure on for that PC to be upgraded - especially as they are migrating from Win 3.11 to Win 95 over the next few weeks.

Molly left about 1 for her train home; Paula and Mary left at about 2. By then, Adele and Kath had arrived. Adele had decided to treat herself to a "posh" hotel in the city centre for the night before flying down to London the next day to see Russel Reid. I phoned Anne and invited her to join Adele, Kym and me for dinner that evening. She already had arrangements for dinner but said she'd try and come round later. Jacqui was also busy that evening.

I still had to get to the supermarket for the evening's supplies. Jacqui arrived just as the other two were leaving - and offered me a lift to the supermarket as her car was outside. As we returned from shopping, we passed Thelma walking back, we obviously stopped to pick her up. (Well, it would have been rude not to as Jacqui was driving Thelma's car!)

They dropped me off and declined an offer of coffee. Much as I love my friends coming round, I was relieved to have a few minutes to myself to just sit and relax before Kym and Adele were due. Well, not so much sit and relax as get the dinner prepared. Kym in fact was due any time.

I had decided to do something very simple - just prepared chicken cordon bleu; baked potatoes and salad - plus garlic bread.

Having organised all of this I got changed. Kym had still not arrived although I had expected her to be here an hour earlier. She did finally turn up. Once Adele arrived, I served dinner. As we were finishing, Anne arrived. After chatting for a while, Anne made some comment about transitioning and Adele's mouth dropped; "I didn't know you were TS" she said "I thought you were an RG".

Anne told us about her recent holiday in Malaga and mentioned that she had the use of the villa again next March and invited me to go with her and some other girls. I'd certainly love to take up the invitation - but my plans are subject to what happens as far as work is concerned. I'll also have to think up some explanation for my wife. I somehow feel that she wouldn't be too happy with the idea of me going with a group of girls. I could tell her that I'm going with a group of friends from the internet - of course - which is perfectly true. Holiday snapshots could pose a potential problem - as will deciding if I'm travelling en-femme or in male mode. I know which I would prefer to do.

Jacqui eventually joined us for coffee. By this time, I have to admit that I was absolutely knackered. Anne offered to drop Adele off at her hotel, leaving Kym and Jacqui at my place; I reluctantly decided at 10.30 that I had to ask them to leave so that I could get to bed.

What a weekend.

Wednesday 12th

Alison was to make her debut this week and came round to the flat to get changed. Julie was also staying the night - so the three of us headed in to the village where we met up with the rest of the regulars. Our tour started in Northern Concord, we then moved on to Paddy's Goose, then round to Churchill's, called into Velvet, Praha, had a glimpse in Via Fosse - then made our way round to Dotz before ending up in Napoleons. As Alison needed to come back to the flat to change back and I wanted to be in bed by midnight, we left naps at about 11.15.

Saturday 15th

Lisa arrived at about 5 - in time for a chat before we changed. We had arranged to meet Kym and Danielle in Paddy's Goose then go on for a meal. Rather than re-visit Via Fosse or Metz, we'd decided to give Praha a try. Unfortunately, by the time we got round there, the chef had left; so, we tried Metz - they couldn't fit us in until 10; Via Fosse was fully booked as well - so we ended up in Velvet. After a 10–15-minute wait, our table was ready for us. The food in Velvet was excellent. The surroundings are not as nice as Via Fosse or Metz - customers have to walk through the dining area to get to the bar so it gets a bit busy.

Before eating, Lisa and I decided to use the loos. There was a queue - and more girls arrived as we were waiting. "Is there a TV in that loo" she asked. "No - but there soon will be" Lisa replied - thinking that the girl had been asking about our sort of TV. She laughed - "Not that sort" she said "I meant a television - on the wall". It appears that one of the cubicles does indeed have a television on the wall!

After eating, we called in at Dotz before ending up, as usual, in Napoleons.

It looks like I may be starting the new year out of work. Unfortunately, I was advised at the end of November that my manager could see no justification for extending my contract as a couple of other projects the company had anticipated had been delayed. I HAVE been told that I would be needed again when these do come on stream - but that won't be before next May (and could be later than that). In the meantime, permanent staff can do the work I was brought in to handle. I guess that's the nature of contracting :-(

But it's not ALL doom and gloom.

Our wonderful TG community has been very supportive. One friend has told me she wants me to produce a corporate web site for her business; another has put me forward for an IT job which could in January and has asked an agency she uses to "look after me" in the meantime; a third has promised me other web production work when her business is launched in a about March; another friend wants some PR doing. Thanks Girls.

Providing I CAN get a reasonably well-paid job by the end of January, things should work out OK. However, I could do with some additional work between Christmas and starting a new full-time job. So, if anyone needs any marketing, publicity, web production or similar work doing - I'd be very interested in hearing about it!

When I phoned my wife to tell her that the contract was likely to end in December, she suggested that I might be better off staying in Manchester as there was probably more temping work up here than at home. That, at least, removed one worry - that of having to return home and give up the flat!

Another problem recently - though not directly affecting me - was the "outing" of a contact of mine from TGFOLK-UK forum and UKTV chat. The Sun newspaper had been tipped off by one of her colleagues about her web site. Angie is an officer with London's Metropolitan Police.

The paper took copies of photographs on the web site together with other information and featured her as the main story on the front page with a double page spread to back it up.

Unfortunately, we do not have privacy laws in the UK so there is no protection against such unwarranted intrusion.

There are, however, copyright laws - and the use, without permission, of photographs from the web site was a clear breach of these laws. What sort of compensation she might get if she were to sue is another matter. Breach of copyright is usually for damages arising from the loss of earnings which might otherwise have been received had the work been paid for. In this case, the press would probably argue that they normally pay a few hundred pounds for freelance photographs and that could be the value assessed. However, as some were used on the front page, that might well be justification for claiming a far higher value. I also heard that in some cases, the claim can take account of the additional profits made from the unauthorised use of copyright material.

Regardless, I have decided to remove my own photo pages and leave only the one picture of me on the introduction. I have also added a warning to my introduction that using any article from my pages is subject to a minimum fee of GB Pounds 100,000 and that the use of anything implies acceptance of those fees.

Well, if a single painting of a vase of flowers can be worth millions - why can't a photo of me? And there are authors who earn millions of pounds/dollars from their writing - again, why not me? If they don't wish to pay that much for my work - fine, then don't publish it!

Frankly, I can think of no reason whatsoever for anyone to want to "out" me. I am not at all in the public eye. But I think it's wise to take sensible precautions without letting the gutter press drive me totally underground!

Now for something completely different.

You'll have seen earlier this month that Kym had arranged to go and see Russell Reid; she was concerned about the possible outcome of this visit in spite of everyone's assurances that she would have no problems with him. I had even said that I would eat one of my wigs if he did not put her on hormones!

My wigs are still intact!

Vanity Club get together in Blackpool

I'd intended taking the afternoon off work to get away early for the weekend, but with the prospect of my contract ending at Christmas, decided I needed to work through to the usual close of business at 3.30.

I returned to the flat to collect my suitcase; quickly checked e-mails in case of any changes to peoples' plans for the weekend and rang Jacqui to let her know I'd pick her up in 5 minutes. "Make it ten" she asked.

I duly arrived outside her flat at ten past four - and waited and waited and waited.

Eventually, the door to the tower block opened and out walked Jacqui accompanied by Thelma - carrying, between them, enough luggage to last a fortnight let alone two nights. I was rather bemused to see Thelma coming with Jacqui as the two hotels we were using were absolutely fully booked. The boot (trunk) of my car was also full with my own suitcase and a toolkit. Where on earth were we going to fit the two of them and their luggage in the car - let alone the hotel?

I went to meet them. "Have we got room?" Jacqui asked. "No" I replied. "It'll all go on the back seat" Jacqui said.

As she packed everything into the car, I realised that all of the luggage was Jacqui's and that Thelma was not joining us.

"What happened to 'just one small case'" I asked.

"Don't ask!" she replied as she got into the front of the car.

As we headed north, she explained that she had been late returning from working in London the previous day and had had no time to select and pack what she wanted - so had brought everything she might need!

The trip to Blackpool was uneventful and we arrived at Lynda's in well under an hour. Most of the others were already there.

I sorted out the final bookings with Lynda - and clarified that a couple of the girls had cancelled, but had been replaced by two others. Lynda told Jacqui and I that we were in another guest house a few doors away and took us down there to meet Barbara, the landlady.

We sorted out who was in which room and learned that we could have accommodated a few more girls as Jacqui's and my rooms had spare beds. Next time we would know. Barbara had never encountered any TVs before - so she was curious about how we would look later.

She found out - and seemed reasonably impressed with our efforts.

We had arranged to meet up in Lynda's and as Jacqui was nowhere near ready - I went up there myself. It was great to meet old friends and some new ones that I'd chatted to on the internet but had not previously met in person - including Kaye and her wife Julie; Kellie Marie's wife Maggie; Gina, a new VC girl from Scotland, Rosemary and Dee.

Gloria and her wife Barbara were due to join us on the Saturday - as was an old friend Deborah.

Having gathered at Lynda's, we ordered taxis to take us to Basil's club. As we were going in, I realised that Anne from Manchester was immediately in front of us. Maybe she'd heard that the VC UK was gathering and had come to Blackpool to avoid us! From Basils, we went on to Lucy's bar, just around the corner.

The evening was fabulous - giving us a chance to get to know each other, have one or two drinks (well, OK - more than one or two), have a dance etc.

When we finally returned to the hotels, I decided not to stay up and chat - otherwise I'd be totally shattered on the Saturday evening. Even so, it was quite late before I got up the next morning and went down to breakfast.

Jacqui was feeling under the weather with a streaming nose - so we left her at Barbara's and went round to Lynda's; several of us walked into town for a lunchtime drink and to do some shopping.

Then it was back to Lynda's to meet the late arrivals before getting ready for another evening on the town!

This started with a meal in Autumn Leaves followed by a short walk around to Flamingos for most of us - with a few of the others heading back to Lucy's.

The evening passed all too quickly and as Flamingo's closed, we ordered five taxis to take us back to Lynda's.

VC UK weekends always pass so quickly. This one had been about the best so far - with several new girls joining the club.

December 1997 — Face to Face in Manchester

The idea of the face-to-face meeting for members of TGFOLK-UK forum had been suggested by Adele when we had been having a meal together in my flat in October.

I'd made the mistake of posting the suggestion on the forum - and had been nominated to organise the event.

With a number of friends offering to accommodate visitors, most of those attending had only to pay travel, meal and drinking costs.

The main logistical problem was that various groups sharing cars for the journey were not necessarily staying at the same place. Kym had invited the younger elements to stay at hers, Pam had asked that only TSs be billeted with her (as it happened, this didn't matter as the vast majority of those coming were TS rather than TV).

The problem was solved (I thought) by using Paddy's Goose as a staging post. BJ and Theresa were travelling up with Rachel G; Paula was collecting Sarah en route and could then take Theresa over to Kym's; Cassie was driving over from Harrogate and could then go on to Pam's with BJ - leaving Rachel to come over to my flat. The others were arriving independently and could go directly to their respective hostesses.

Fine in principle - then we heard that Cassie's car had been stolen that morning.

OK - so Cassie can come to my place and Rachel can take BJ on to Pam's and stay there. Problem solved.

Err, not quite. Rachel, Theresa and BJ were late arriving - by which time Kym and Paula had left Paddy's Goose. So, Rachel brought Theresa and BJ round to my flat - she could then go on to Pam's with BJ. Well, she could have done if she hadn't been so totally shattered from the long drive. As she wasn't interested in the clubbing on the Friday evening, she said she would just get a takeaway and get to bed early.

OK - so that left BJ, Theresa and myself to head into the village; my other guests were expected to arrive late in any case. As we were about to leave the flat, Wendy arrived. She had a few seconds to bring in her things - but no time to change for the evening. She gallantly offered to drive us into the Village - so off we went.

The other groups met up with us in PG - plus a few local girls joining us for the evening; then it was round to Churchill's for a drink, down Canal Street to show them other Village venues like Praha, Bar 38 and Via Fosse before making our way to Dotz - then finally on to Napoleons.

We called it a night relatively early (1ish) and headed back to the various billets.

On the Saturday, most of the groups met up for lunch in PG - then headed for the shops; Rachel G, Theresa and Sarah had been persuaded to have their ears pierced - and most wanted to pick up a few bits and pieces.

As we wandered around the shops, the groups gradually broke up but we all eventually met up again at PG in time to head back to get changed for the evening.

Back in the village once more, I had a nervous 45 minutes collecting the balances of the meal costs - but eventually ended up with just one "no show".

We then left Paddy's and walked around to Metz - where there were bottles of wine waiting for us on the table courtesy of Metz and Dotz. Thanks Chris!

I didn't hear any complaints at all about the food - and when the waiters started to dance on the tables...........

After Metz we went round to Dotz - with a few others heading straight for Napoleons. It was at Dotz that we had what could have been a very serious problem. Natalie was not feeling well so she went outside; Jacqui had just got her sitting in the car when some lunatic jumped in and drove off down the road with Natalie. Fortunately, he stopped - and Jacqui was able to take Natalie to the hospital. Equally fortunately, it seems that there was nothing seriously wrong with her and she was released later.

Most of us were unaware of the drama that had unfolded until much later.

Unfortunately, the night was soon over.

Sunday saw a final gathering in PG to switch cars again for the journeys home. That evening on UKTV, many of the girls put in an appearance and made those who had been unable to attend very very jealous with their stories of the weekend.

The consensus was that it had been brilliant! AND that it HAD to be repeated.

Cassie and Kym volunteered to take on the next one!

I think the idea is for it to be in March!

January 1998 — RIP Alexandra

I had some extremely sad news this month.

Alex, one of the girls who helped me so very much when I first joined the Internet was killed in a road accident. She and Ralph had only recently married - doing so in France where post op TSs are able to do so.

I never actually met or spoke to Alex other than through the net - but I shall miss her. I have met Ralph several times and my heart goes out to him. They both deserved so much more than just a few short months together.

Other news in my December Diary, I mentioned that I had been advised that my contract would probably end at Christmas. In spite of attempts to get it extended, it did, indeed end on Christmas Eve. I was, however, assured that I would be asked back as soon as some projects which had been delayed went ahead. This could be anytime from now until next summer. In the meantime, I shall be staying in Manchester.

I've had a heck of a lot of support from my TG friends - both TVs and TSs. I've been put forward for jobs with their companies, been offered freelance work from several sources, friends who used to crash at my flat free of charge now insist on contributing to my funds. I have to say that I am humbled by all of the help I've been offered.

Frann features rather heavily in the diary for the end of December and beginning of January.

She first came up to Manchester about a month ago. Unfortunately, due to circumstances, this initial visit was not the success that she had hoped. I had an e-mail from her soon afterwards explaining why she had been disappointed. I was dismayed - not because I had been responsible for her disappointment, but because I felt she had been let down by others.

I was determined to put things right!

Paula (Paula UK on Donna's Den) planned to come up to spend New Year with me. "Can you pick up Frann on the way," I asked. "Of course." Replied Paula (as I knew she would). It was arranged. They would come up on New Year's Eve. Then I had a message - could they come up the day before. "YES" I said.

Then Paula contacted me on the Monday. "Sorry, but I can't make it after all". I contacted Frann and explained the situation and told her that she was still welcome to come if she could make it by public transport. She said she'd check and advise whether she'd be coming by coach or train.

Paula called again at 10 that night. She had decided to come after all. "Now?" I asked. "As soon as I finish my evening job" she replied. It's a three-hour drive from her house to Manchester so she'd be arriving about 2.30-3am. "No problem, I don't have to get up early for work" I said. She told me that she had tried to phone Frann but that her line was busy and suggested that I check on IRC to see if she was chatting on UKTV. She was. I messaged her - she responded by saying she'd sorted out the travel arrangements for the next day. Forget it, I told her - can you be ready in 90 minutes - Paula's on her way! "Yeeeeeeeaaaaaaahhhh" was the reply "I'm ready now".

They actually arrived at 3.30am. We stayed up and chatted 'til 6 - then decided that we'd better get some sleep ready for the evening ahead.

New Year's Eve was fabulous - what I remember of it anyway. We visited Paddy's Goose, Dotz, and Napoleons - then went back to Sal & Martin's house. I'd had more than my usual to drink and ended up in a spare bed for a while!

On New Year's Day, Paula had to return home. Frann was packed ready to go when I reiterated an invitation to stay on for a few days. She rapidly unpacked again.

We went out again on the Friday and Saturday evenings.

On the Saturday we had a trip to Blackpool for the evening - resulting in 6 girls stopping at the flat.

Last Thursday, Frann came back up to Manchester and stayed until Sunday morning. - we spent Friday shopping en femme in Manchester city centre. We parked the car in the Village and walked over to the Arndale centre.

I'd seen a gorgeous blue dress in C&A on a previous visit and wanted to see if they still had it. Unfortunately, they did not; but there was another dress which caught my eye. As it was an 18 (US 22) and I usually take 20 (though I've been losing weight consistently) - I decided to try it on. No problem, I waited 'til the changing rooms were relatively quiet and just walked over and asked - the girl gave me a tag and I went into one of the cubicles. Unfortunately, the dress was just a bit too tight - so I left it with the girl. Frann bought a couple of items.

We then went to the market and visited the Sparklers stall. Vicky recognised me from Northern Concord events and we had a chat and I bought a couple of inexpensive rings while Frann bought a teddy bear brooch. As we left the market a couple of teenage girls passed us and one said to the other "look a couple of trannies" - Frann just turned to them, smiled and said "that's right". We went over to Affleck's Palace (a shopping centre full of stalls selling "alternative" clothing and accessories), had a coffee & a snack, then explored the stalls.

Frann needed some more shoes so we returned to the car and drove round to Shoe City.

We found that they had about 6-8 styles in our size (we both take 10 - 10 1/2). Tried on all that we could find in our sizes. We both selected what we wanted and went to pay for them.

The girl on the checkout turned out to be one of the staff from Saxones who used to open late for NC members - so we had a pleasant chat with her and no embarrassment whatsoever paying using our male cash cards.

We then decided to go and visit Transformation (for a laugh). We walked in and I said to the girl on the counter "Frann wants a change-away - she wants to spend the afternoon as a boy!" The girl just smiled and offered us a coffee.

Now for a confession.

We then started looking at the sale items - and, horror of horrors, there were actually some things being sold off at reasonable prices. I am utterly ashamed to admit that I tried on a suit (jacket and skirt) and bought it. OK - it was very nice and ideal for business meetings en femme (I've been doing some freelance work for a TS friend); it was also just £20. But how can I hold my head up again in the Village?????

After Transformation, we went to do some food shopping at my local supermarket. This included asking for some bacon, ham and cheese.

There were one or two glances - but no-one took any significant notice of either of us. Considering that I am size 20 and 5'10" and Frann is well over 6', we are not typical female sizes.

Whether I shall get any comments from the staff next time I go there in male mode remains to be seen - I shop there at least once a week :)

Last night btw, Frann, Kath and I went out for a meal at a straight pub/restaurant in Stoke on Trent (well - Newcastle under Lyme to be precise – which is where my father was born).

There were one or two sniggers and looks from a handful of the other diners but no overt comments or any unpleasantness.

So, overall, I've had a very pleasant start to '98 in spite of being unemployed.

What lies ahead? Who knows? Come back and find out.

February 1998

I am still looking for work. I've had a few leads but nothing permanent at present.

Friends have gathered around - and when visitors come to stay, they nearly all insist on giving me something towards expenses. I've also been taken out to dinner a few times while taking new girls or old friends around the village.

As a consequence of my unemployed status, I am currently able to dress virtually full time. In fact, apart from shopping (and not always then) or other occasions, such as job interviews/ meetings, when male dress is more appropriate, I spend all of my time en femme. I estimate that the maximum time I've been in male mode since Boxing Day is 7 hours and that the total works out to an average of less than an hour a day.

I feel so totally "natural" en femme. Yet have no problems reconciling myself to periods when male clothes are more appropriate.

I am spending a fair bit of my time experimenting with web page production - learning new HTML editing tools such as Hot Dog and Corel Webmaster.

We had a VC UK weekend at Lisa's in Norwich on 7th/8th February. Lisa had had a cycling accident on that Saturday which left her legs badly grazed and meant that she had to give up her usual miniskirt for trousers.

The weekend marked the transfer of the Presidency of Vanity Club UK from Lisa to me. I had been extremely flattered to have been asked to take over the reins.

Stephanie from Norwich has agreed to act as my Vice President and Lisa will be our ambassadrix to VC US.

The Vanity Club UK pages have now been transferred to Geocities - and updated. If you are interested in membership, or even if you are not, take a look at them.

March 1998

The work situation is still pretty much the same - a few leads, especially for future freelance work but nothing permanent at present.

I said last month that I'm spending most of my time en femme. Not a subtle change there. Last month I referred to it as being dressed. Having spent nearly 3 months almost totally femme, I'm not sure I consider being en femme as "dressing" any longer. It's now my normal state. I calculated that since Christmas, I've spent about 3% of my time in "male mode" - and I now feel that I am "dressing" when I wear my male shoes, jacket and jeans and go out without make up. I also said "I feel so totally "natural" en femme. Yet have no problems reconciling myself to periods when male clothes are more appropriate."

Hmm. I'm not sure that this is necessarily true any longer. I do think "yeauk" when I have to go out in male mode. Even when I'm dressed male, I still wear my femme panties, T shirt and knee-highs - my jeans are androgynous and the shoes I use are Cuban heeled boots (the heels are about 2").

In fact, apart from a very few occasions when being en femme might cause problems - eg visiting the employment office - the only reason I don't dress 100% is because I've been getting rid of my facial hair recently and need to have stubble for a few days at a time. THIS does cause me to feel decidedly un-femme. (Can't say it makes me feel male - because it doesn't. I really don't feel masculine these days - and don't miss that side at all).

I wondered in the past if I'd get fed up of being en femme. Would I want to dress in male mode just for a change? The answer is "not at all". I have started wondering just how significant this might be.

My own hair is now almost long enough to wear in a short feminine style - another few weeks and I'll probably have it styled and, perhaps, coloured. My nails are now long enough not to need to wear false ones.

The face as mentioned earlier, I've been trying to get rid of my facial hair. I'd thought about conventional electrolysis - but the time involved and cost put me off. I also considered laser electrolysis - but, again, the cost is prohibitive at the moment. I'd tried once before to use an epilator on my face - it had been very painful, but the small area I'd treated had never regrown. I decided to try to clear the whole beard area.

One of the advantages I have being out of work is being able to let my stubble grow without getting comments about looking scruffy. The downside is that I can't go out femme with stubble!

I let the hair grow for 48 hours so that the epilator would have something to grab. Mistake. BIG MISTAKE!

The hair was relatively dense - so there were plenty for the epilator to catch - and it did; and it hurt. OW - did it hurt! I persevered - trying to nibble at the edges of the growth area.

I kept this up for a few days - having a go every few hours. I then had to shave off the rest in order to go out.

I usually go out on Saturdays and Wednesdays; this means shaving those evenings and allows Sunday- Wed and Thurs - Sat for the hairs to grow.

For the next session, I didn't leave it as long, realising that the hairs were growing at different rates and if I started earlier, less hairs would be long enough to be caught. It was still painful, but tolerable for far longer at a time. During this session, I still wasn't clearing all of the hairs which were long enough - so as the series of clearances went on, more and more hairs were being caught. I eventually gave up on that session!

Subsequent sessions became gradually easier as the hairs were thinned out. Now it's down to less than 10% of the original density it's almost like using an electric shaver - with just the occasional sharp tug as a tough root is removed.

Obviously, the roots are not being destroyed and the hairs should regrow eventually - but as they are on about an 8–13-week cycle, I should be dealing with 5-8% of the original levels at any time because I'll be catching the new hairs as they emerge. I HOPE that continued removal of roots will weaken them - that's been suggested as likely.

Ultimately, I plan to have laser treatment. As the hairs are far less dense, this should be far less painful than if I had done nothing. I'd anticipate needing at least 3 face clearances using laser. One disadvantage I've been warned of using the epilator is that the roots are likely to be distorted and conventional electrolysis could be problematical.

The reality is that I look like having cleared almost all of my facial hairs within a couple of months for minimal cost (I already had the epilator, but even if I hadn't, the cost would have been less than a couple of sessions of electrolysis). Yes, it's been painful - but so is electrolysis whether conventional or laser. I anticipate being told off when I eventually go for other treatment - but it seems to have been effective for me.

What else have I been up to?

There are a couple of other projects I've been working on which also look quite promising - and can be done en-femme.

If these come off, I may well be able to forget about going back to a full-time male mode job!

That would be a dream come true!

It would, of course, raise some other questions. I'm honestly not sure what I would do about coming out to my wife and daughter. I rather suspect I'd have to sooner or later as I'd continue growing my hair and nails and wouldn't wish to cut them just for occasional trips home.

Would I want to take any further steps towards possible transition?

I really don't know. I suspect that would depend on family reactions if I decided to come out. If there was acceptance of a femme lifestyle without further feminisation beyond facial hair and nails - then I suspect that's as far as I would go. If they can't even accept my transvestism and current lifestyle and we split up, then I suspect that the brakes would be well and truly "off" and I could well see me taking further steps.

We shall have to wait and see.

May 1998

Monday 18th May didn't quite go as planned.

I've been trying to get a transfer from my current flat to one in a tower block with secure parking as there have been seven attacks on my car and those of visitors within a year. I also need a larger flat to accommodate all the girls who visit me from time to time. (There are plenty of vacant council properties in Salford). The council housing department had advised me that there was a blanket ban on moves - but I'd also been advised that individual cases could be reconsidered and I've been trying to persuade them to do so in my case.

My bathroom had some mould in the corners of the walls and ceilings from drying very wet laundry one day without adequate ventilation - so I decided to strip the wallpaper in the affected area and repaint that part. (I'd actually cleared the mould - but it had left stain marks on the wallpaper) I knew that under "Sod's Law", if I started to do this, the chances were that the council would agree to a move to make the exercise pointless.

I was dressed in scruffy femme mode (top, grotty leggings that show every bulge, hair held back in a headband, nail varnish on, boobs in place - thick rubber gloves to protect my hands - what a sight!). The bathroom window was well open and I could see the entrance to the flats.

I'd been working for about 2 hours and was extremely sweaty when I noticed a man approaching the flats. He didn't ring any of the bells so I assumed he had moved in upstairs.

A few minutes later, there was a knock at my door. I opened it on the chain and the guy I'd noticed was standing there. He was from the council and had come round to discuss my application for a transfer. :-)

I said "You'd better come in - but be ready for a shock".

I showed him into the lounge and he asked if it was a bad time. Bit of an understatement!

He didn't really bat an eyelid about my appearance. I had actually planned to go down the housing office en femme to add weight to my application for a move from a vulnerable ground floor flat to one in a tower block on the grounds that my lifestyle could attract problems from bigots. I think having him turn up and seeing me probably carried more weight as it might have seemed like a put-up job if I'd just gone along to the housing office en femme. At least he saw that this IS the way I live these days.

The outcome of his visit was that he will recommend that my application for a transfer should be approved.

I then had a phone call from an RG friend asking if I fancied going shopping with her. As I needed to get the paint for the bathroom, I agreed. She then came back to my flat for a coffee afterwards.

She was about to leave when I had a phone call from another friend telling me to put the kettle on as they were about 5 minutes away.

I'd intended to get on with the redecorating that evening but we went down the Village for a bite to eat and ended up chatting til 4am.

I decided the next day to post a message to TGFolk-UK forum about the visit from the Council official - I thought it would amuse my friends on the list!

Claire - a TS - replied:

Really, Helen, you could save yourself a lot of grief, not to say the confusion engendered (pun intended) in your pals, if you went whole hog and joined me in having a little [snip]

After all, how can you ever turn up at the Northern Concord again after coughing (police term for admitting) that you were seen wearing that outfit? Now anyone that knows anything knows that no self-respecting TV or TG would ever be seen dead in an outfit like that. Only TS that have had their dress sense removed at the same time as the [snip] would even consider it.

Oh hell, good on yer girl! I wished I had seen that council bloke's face - I'll bet his day was not quite as planned as well. :)

The reply had me in stiches! (Even without any snips!)

As regular visitors to my pages will know, my attitude to being TV or TS has been shifting over the last year or so. My theory on what makes us TV or TS fits in with these changing feelings. I decided to post another message in response to Claire's comments:

On a serious note, the fact that I do spend virtually all my time as Helen these days has, naturally, made me wonder where my future lies.

I am beginning to accept that transition is probably inevitable for me. (Isn't that a BIG surprise for those who know me? Probably about as unexpected as the election result last year).

So why do I hesitate?

SC said in her posting on "decisions":

"I think the biggest problem that I generally face is the "fear", though I don't think it has every stopped me, only delayed things until the forward push exceeds the backwards fear."

I can certainly empathise with this view.

There are still factors holding me back. Some major, some trivial.

I am totally comfortable as Helen. I much prefer being Helen. Almost all of my friends ONLY know me as Helen. I even have several non-T* friends (male and female) who only see me and relate to me as female.

There are very few things that I now do in male mode and these are growing fewer and fewer. Even these are done generally in androgynous mode rather than fully male.

It would be so easy for me to say - "I might just as well go the whole way". But this is, I believe, a totally inappropriate reason. I still do certain things in male mode which I

COULD do en femme - and don't feel wrong or even uncomfortable in that role (though I do now see it as a role rather than my natural state).

I do have a programme for myself. That is to eliminate all of the factors that I can which would present problems should I decide to transition: facial hair, nails, hair, employment, my weight and smoking.

I had believed that medical reasons could present problems - being overweight and family history (my father died of heart attack and my mother also has angina) suggested that I could have had blood pressure and I suspected that my cholesterol levels might have been high - but I recently registered with a new doctor up here and had a complete medical which showed that I was within acceptable limits and had no other problems.

(I had been quite concerned that I might decide to transition and then find that medical reasons would prevent me from doing so. That does not now appear to be a problem).

I am also waiting until I feel uncomfortable in male role - rather than just preferring to be Helen. If that happens, then I shall know that transition is right for me. By then, hopefully, the outstanding "problems" will only be the effect on my family. Not that I am implying that these would be trivial - of course they are not!

My wife and I have not lived together now for 3 years due to my previous work contracts and we have mutually concluded that there is little prospect or wish for us to get back together.

My daughter will be 21 this year and will either accept me or not.

My mother is a more significant problem. She is 75 and has angina and other medical problems - In spite of which she leads an active life and is completely mentally alert. But I know what her reaction used to be to transvestism. I would hate to be responsible for adding stress which could cause more problems for her. If I need to proceed - then telling her would be the biggest worry for me.

I also have a sister - who I rarely see. She and I are far from close - though our relationship is amicable enough.

I never wanted to be TS. I certainly do not see it as a goal - or being the "ultimate" in terms of T*ism. IF I decide that it is right for me - then it will be because I can no longer accept switching between roles.

I will, as I have suggested before, be a failed transvestite.

There is a verse in "Some Days are Diamonds (Some Days are Stone)" on a John Denver CD which reflects my current position (it's playing as I write this posting):

...now the face in the mirror more and more is a stranger to me, more and more I can see there's a danger in becoming what I never thought I'd be.

I DO look in the mirror when male mode and see someone who I "used to know". And I certainly see myself becoming something I never thought I would be.

I don't feel worried by this prospect as such - only the consequences of that step. I also want to be absolutely certain that if I do go further that it is for the right reason.

I said last year that it was my view that the root cause of all T*ism was the same; that the force that this creates varied and was countered by conditioning and other braking forces; that these braking forces tended to diminish over time. I said that it was my view that when the net force reached a certain level - then the individual would be TV, if the net force was significantly higher, then only full transition would suffice. I suggested that this could explain why some TVs apparently became TS - and why some secondary TSs emerged later in life following major reductions in braking forces.

My braking forces are diminishing week by week - and I am finding my net driving force increasing. I need to be 100% certain that any decision to proceed further is based on a genuine need and not because of any possibility that I am fulfilling my own predictions and theories.

I used to wonder if I'd become bored with being en femme given an opportunity to do so every day. After 5 months of living 95% en femme I think I can conclude that this is not the case. I find it quite natural to get up and dress as Helen.

I believe that I know exactly where I stand at present. I'm not putting off making any decision - I am waiting for the appropriate conditions to be met before accepting that I need to take further action. If (when) those conditions are met - then I will know what to do. I'm certainly not going to push myself. Nor am I going to set myself any deadlines.

With all of my TS friends, I have a pretty good idea what to expect. I'm certainly not looking forward to the prospect of the downsides of the treatment - and the thought of surgery is far from attractive. But these factors won't hold me back if/when I decide the time is right.

June 1998

After the revelations in May, what can June hold?

Well - I'm getting closer and closer to telling my wife and daughter that I am TV.

A group of us went to the Rocky Horror show a few weeks ago. This was at a theatre not far from the Village.

When I next spoke to my wife on the phone, I told her that I had been. She was amazed that I had done so; but didn't ask many questions and accepted my explanation that it was 60's music which she knows I enjoy.

My daughter, on the other hand, having expressed similar surprise, asked if I'd dressed up for it?

"What do you think?" I asked her.

"No" she replied dejectedly.

"Wrong" I told her

"WHAT?" she exclaimed in an amazed tone. "Stockings and suspenders and all that?"

"Yes" I replied "you have to enter into the spirit of these things don't you!"

She was utterly amazed at my revelation.

"Just shows - your old man isn't such a boring "stick in the mud" after all is he?"

"Err - no, I guess not" she replied.

The next time I spoke to my wife, she said: "You didn't tell me that you had dragged up for the Rocky Horror Show".

"You didn't ask" I pointed out.

"Were any photos taken?"

"Yes"

"I'll have to see them, then" she said.

That's not the only ones she is likely to see!

The ground has now been prepared for the revelation! OK there is a very big difference between seeing a pic of me dressed for the RHS - and dressed as I usually go down the Village - but it does provide an opening.

When will I tell her? Soon. I'm seeing her on 8th July for our daughter's university graduation ceremony. That won't be the time to do it - I have no intention of "raining on her parade" - but it will certainly be as soon afterwards as I can manage.

Other incidents this month: I was giving an RG friend of mine a lift to hospital for some tests. Just after picking her up, I had a flat tyre. I got the spare and jack out of the boot and started to replace the wheel. A woman pedestrian walked past us "Nice to see ladies who can handle their own car problems" she remarked.

At the hospital, I stayed in the waiting room while Gilda had the first of the tests - involving a tube being inserted into her nostril - then down her throat into the stomach. Not nice! Gilda then came into the waiting room for a break before the next procedure. She asked if I could sit with her while it was done; the nurse said that would be fine.

This involved a smaller tube being inserted in the same way as the first.

As the nurse was getting ready to proceed, Gilda apologised for any fuss she had made during the first stage. The nurse said not to worry and that she had been far better than most men who have the same test done - then started to berate "macho guys" for their nervousness and reaction to the test. This while I am sitting 3 feet from her. Either the nurse was just totally blasé about me or she hadn't realised that I am TV.

I collect my mail for Vanity Fair from a sorting office near my flat. I used to change into male mode when doing so; but recently I've been going over en femme. Last Thursday, I was going to the bank immediately afterwards so went over in male mode. "Where's your dress today?" asked the girl on the desk!

Back to Work as a male! I heard a couple of weeks ago from my previous company that they have now been awarded one of the contracts they'd been expecting. My old manager there rang to ask if I was available and interested in going back.

Whilst the thought of reverting to male mode to work is far from appealing, I do need the cash so I said yes.

That is going to be a very interesting test for me when it comes. It may well answer some questions about my future!

Moving Flat I've also been advised that there is a vacancy in the block of flats I want to move to and invited to view the place.

Things seem to be happening in a number of ways!

Come back and see what happens next.

July 1998

I'm actually writing this diary for July well into August.

I said in June that I was getting closer to telling my wife and daughter that I am TV. I also mentioned that I had been offered a flat in a tower block just up the road - and that I had been contacted regarding possible work.

The work has not come through - but the move did.

I didn't tell my wife and daughter anything during July. We all met up for my daughter's graduation - but, just in case the revelation went badly, I decided it was not the right occasion to say anything. I had no intention of spoiling her day.

We did all arrange to meet at my wife's house at the beginning of August. I resolved to make my announcements there. Would I chicken out at the last minute? You'll have to go to next month's diary to find the answer.

I had also decided, in any case, that there was little point in remaining married. My wife has her life and friends where she lives; I have mine in Manchester. We've lived apart for more than 3 years and had touched on the subject of getting back together last time we had met. It had been apparent from that conversation that neither of us really wanted to live together again. There is no animosity - just a matter of us having drifted apart over 30 years.

As I mentioned above, the flat move came through in the middle of the month. The one I was offered was on the twelfth floor of the tower block. With quite a few other trannies living there, the security guards are well used to seeing us. I was already a regular visitor to the block in any case.

Apart from the usual hassle of moving, especially getting everything up in the lift (elevator) and into the actual rooms from the hallway (one wardrobe had to be dismantled), and the inevitable breaking of a few nails, it all went relatively smoothly.

The following weekend, we had a Vanity Club UK gathering in Blackpool which was well attended.

August 1998

I arrived "home" early afternoon after a fairly tiring drive.

After initial greetings and being provided with a cup of coffee, the subject of the Rocky Horror photographs was raised. See Coming out to Jo and Jenny for how it went.

I was actually amazed at the reaction I received - or lack of it. Both were extremely understanding of the situation - and seemed reasonably well informed. I am quite certain the fact that my wife and I were splitting up in any case helped her to accept my position and I have no doubt that if we had been trying to hold the marriage together then the outcome might have been different. I suspect that she would have accepted my need to dress - providing it was not around the house or local area.

My daughter later asked if I planned to have other relationships and said that she thought I should.

My wife agreed that there was no reason to tell her parents or family that I was TV - and that she didn't see any reason for me to tell my mother or sister at present and she wouldn't mention it either. Obviously, we have told the family about the separation. Nobody has been surprised about that.

Quite a weekend!

September/ October 1998

I have been rather busy recently - which is why there has been a break in my diary. It's not that there has been nothing to say - just too little time to write it!

In Mid- August, about a week after the last update, I was offered work. This was in a PC workshop - upgrading, repairing and renovating machines. When the agency contacted me, they implied that it was long term. When I arrived at the workshop, I found I was covering for another engineer who had been seconded to another site but was expected back within a couple of weeks. This wasn't exactly good news for me as I would hardly break even on such a short-term assignment. It would, however "show willing" for the employment centre!

Not viewing the placement as long term probably led me to do something I might otherwise have avoided! I came out to the supervisor as TV after comments he made about drag queens. See "Coming Out At Work".

He and I will continue to disagree on basics - but it looks like we can live with each other's' honestly held beliefs.

One of the other activities which delayed the updating of my diary is a counselling course I've registered for. It's only a 12 week "Introduction to Counselling" - but could, over the next 4 years lead to a Diploma in Counselling involving one evening a week at Salford University.

I only enrolled in time for the second evening - at which the tutor asked us all to say something about an item we were wearing or had with us and what it said about us. I'd gone almost straight from work - so was dressed rather casually in jeans, sweatshirt etc. As the others had their say, I wondered what I could say about myself.

Swallowing a lump in my throat, I said that my name was Mike - at least that was one of the names I use and that I was dressed casually because I liked to feel comfortable - and that the reason I was on the course was to learn more about counselling because of a section of the community that I was a member of that I wanted to help feel comfortable with what they are. I said they would probably have seen an example of this on Coronation Street - Hayley. I said the people I wanted to help were transsexual individuals and transvestites. I told them that I was also known as Helen.

You could have heard a pin drop. The reaction I've had since then has been quite positive - but I'd have been very disappointed if there had been any negative reaction from people training to be counsellors of course.

One evening we had a session of role playing - one acting as a "client" the other as "counsellor". My partner was in fact the tutor. I decided to have some fun with her! Before this session started the tutor took the other "counsellors" to one side to brief them on how to behave during the "session".

I used a genuine example from someone I have tried to help.

I have to say that the tutor was totally beaten by the challenge I presented her with. She had no idea of how to cope with the problem of a Transsexual person. She even forgot to try to "throw me" with the reaction she had briefed the other counsellors with!

In the end she admitted that she would not know where to start if faced with the problem I had given her. I pointed out that I had some experience of the practical aspects of helping TVs and TSs - but was very conscious of my lack of training in counselling and that's why I was on the course. I also said that if she did encounter TVs/ TSs - then I could point them in the right directions and she said she would follow up on that if the situation arose.

November/ December 1998

I appear to be heading for a crisis.

As you will have seen from earlier diary entries, I have outed myself to my wife and daughter, friends and colleagues. The one person I have been trying to protect has been my mother - and, because of this, I had tried to keep the news of my transgenderism from my sister. It wasn't that I didn't trust my sister not to tell our mother - but there is always the possibility of accidentally letting something slip which then results in awkward questions. I was also conscious that if my sister knew, then she would share the responsibility of keeping the news from mother.

My wife and I are separating/ divorcing quite amicably. I had told her about my new lifestyle so that she understood why I was prepared to accept the end of our marriage - and to avoid the need for our daughter to have to keep quiet about my TGism. (I felt I had to tell her as she is quite likely to visit me in Manchester at some stage and would be faced with my new home being rather un-masculine).

By telling both of them, I felt that each could talk to the other and share any "problems" they might have with my TGism. As it happens, neither appeared to have any difficulty accepting that I was TG.

At least, that's what I thought at the time.

My wife had agreed not to tell her parents nor my sister about me. (Her mother talks to my mother and I had no confidence that she would be able to keep quiet about my situation if she knew about it).

A couple of weeks ago, I received a letter from my wife stating that she could no longer agree to keep the news from her parents. It appears that they have been trying to persuade her not to go through with the divorce. Obviously, the fact that I am TG is a factor as she would not be happy if we were living together and I was going in and out of the house dressed.

Later that same day, I received a cryptic message on my answering service from my sister asking me to call her. When I did so, she asked if there was something I needed to tell her. I played ignorant - and asked what she was on about; she said she had written me a letter and I would have to wait until I received it.

Suspecting that my wife might have told my sister, I tried phoning her. Later that day, I eventually got in touch with my wife and asked if she had said anything about me to my sister. Her silence told me that she had and, when I prompted her further, she admitted that she had told my sister that I was TS.

The letter from my sister arrived a few days later. It was much more supportive than I felt it would be from the tone of our telephone conversation - and I then called her and explained what I could. I told her why I had not previously confided in her and said I would prefer to talk about things face to face and invited her to come up to Manchester. She asked if the invitation included her partner and I said it did; and that I would also probably have a new partner with me. I explained to her that I now have a girlfriend in Manchester. As I did not want my wife to feel that as soon as we had separated, I had found a replacement for her, I asked my sister not to tell her about Gilda. She said she would not deliberately reveal the news - but nor would she lie if asked directly. She said the same situation applied to telling our mother about me. She did, at least agree to let me know if she did tell either of them.

If the news is going to come out - then it absolutely has to be from me and not any other source.

I am encouraged by a recent telephone conversation with my mother. During it she hinted that she knows that there is something about my lifestyle in Manchester; she has seen my longer, dyed hair and may have noticed other things about me. (My sister certainly had).

However, my mother has said that she has noticed that I am far happier in myself these days and whilst she may put this down substantially to Gilda, she has also said that we all have to live our own lives and I get the impression that she will support me regardless.

I still don't want to cause her any distress.

Even if she can accept the fact that I am potentially TS, I can't help wondering if she might feel in some way responsible for this.

Certainly, she might well feel guilty for the fact that I have been unable to accept my condition for so many years. I suspect it's a no-win situation.

I suspect that if I tell her, she will be upset either because of what I am - or because of the guilt and shame I carried for so long.

If I don't tell her and she hears it from someone else - then she will be even more upset.

As said at the beginning of this entry, it looks like crisis time in the new year. I am sure we will get through it - but not without some pain.

Other news is that I am still currently employed. Whether this will continue after Xmas has not yet been confirmed but the indications look reasonable.

The best news from this year, however, is GILDA.

I've known Gilda for about three years - since soon after going out regularly in the Village in fact. We had often been part of the same crowd - and we gradually became friends. We would joke together. Occasionally dance with each other. She came back to my flat one evening with a crowd. Unfortunately, she has a medical condition which is affected by drinking and smoking and results in attacks which are extremely painful for her for an hour or so. I'd previously seen the result of one such attack while she was in the Village. This particular evening, she had such an attack while at my flat and I put her in my bed while her medication took effect. Samantha remained with her and held her hand until the attack subsided. By the time Gilda had recovered, nearly everyone else had left.

Some of the girls were stopping over - which meant that the lounge was full and the only place left for me to sleep was in the same bed as Gilda. As I joined her, she turned to me and asked what we were doing in bed together. I told her that as long as she didn't try to take advantage of me - she was welcome to stay. She hit me! As it happens, I had no intention of letting anything happen between us and, in any case, she had to get back to her own house to be there for her two girls the next morning (they were sleeping over at friends). I called a taxi for her and she left.

We met up several times after this before anything actually happened between us. But, once it did, our relationship grew stronger and stronger. Her two girls and most of her family accept me as Helen.

Where this will lead remains to be seen. We are both well aware that if I decide to go further, then things may change between us. We are also realistic enough to realise that whilst WE would probably be very happy together in a lesbian relationship, it may well present problems for her family - just as my own condition might pose problems with my mother.

We are, therefore, taking steps one at a time.

As far as I am concerned, I would have to judge whether the overall quality of my life would be devalued by going further than I am at present. I know I feel far better when I am Helen than in male mode. At present, I can cope with having to be male sometimes - eg at work. The relationship with Gilda makes an immensely positive contribution to that quality of life and I have to balance the possible loss of this (and other factors) against the ability to transition fully and finally become the person I really am. If I can get the best of both worlds, then that would, of course, be ideal.

I am still taking steps to prepare for possible full transition.

I have just started laser electrolysis. I am aware of the comparative claims of conventional electrolysis and laser treatment. My therapist is, however, confident that laser treatment is as effective as conventional methods - and she used to do conventional electrolysis. We shall see.

I think I mentioned in earlier diaries that I have recently been taking a training course in counselling. I believe that there is a significant need for counsellors to support TGs - whether TV or TS. As I have had some reasonable success in helping others, I am hopeful of developing this side. If this does work, it might provide a possible career move which would obviously be possible post-transition.

Thursday 17th December was, the final evening of the introductory course. I had been attending the course in male mode as I had been going straight from work. On the penultimate evening, I had asked the tutor if she had any problem with me coming to the final evening as Helen. She had assured me that she would be very happy for me to do so.

I left work early to allow time to change then get over to the college.

What should I wear? In point of fact, the previous few weeks, I'd been wearing female jeans and tops and Cuban heeled boots which were androgynous. I considered wearing the same - but with my boobs in place, hair in a feminine style and make up and jewellery; after some thought I rejected the casual look. I decided that I wanted to look smart - but not overdressed. I chose a burgundy, button through, dress which is just below knee length, a scarf which helps with the rather deep V neck and smart 3-inch-high court shoes.

I had a quick bath - then got made up and dressed and did my hair. How does that look I wondered? A glance in the mirror showed that I had done a reasonable job!

As I approached the door to the building housing our classroom, I saw Ros - one of my fellow students having a smoke before class. He glanced at me as I approached - then looked away again. As I reached him, I said "Hi!". A look of astonishment appeared on his face!

Several of the other students complimented me on my appearance "You look fabulous" said one! During the course of the evening, Anne, the tutor, said that she had felt "chuffed" that I had felt able to attend as Helen. At the end, she gave me a hug and wished me the best of luck for the future. She even offered to have my certificate for the course made out for "Helen Williamson" rather than the name under which I had enrolled.

1998 is now drawing to a close. In spite of the fact that I was out of work for eight months, it's been a terrific year for me. Yes, there have been problems. I lost a couple of friends in the summer - one through my own thoughtlessness, which I still regret very much. The other through a misunderstanding which we have now put behind us. But overall, I think I may well look back on '98 as a watershed. If 1999 is half as good to me, then I shall be approaching the new millennium with confidence.

Another important factor at this time is reflecting on some of the other girls I've been in touch with over the past twelve months or so. A year ago, I had reason to be extremely concerned for two or three of them. I am delighted that one in particular has ended 1998 in a far more positive frame of mind than she started it

Christmas/ New Year 1998/9

My diary has not been updated for several months. In fact, I thought I had added the events of Christmas and New Year - but, whilst I did post a brief summary to TG Folk Forum, it appears that I forgot to update my own diary. My excuse is that things have been rather hectic since then.

Anyway, here goes with the update - which is effectively a reprint of the posting to TG Folk:

Christmas & New Year certainly saw some ups and downs for me.

My daughter and her fiancé came over for New Year's Eve. Joanna had seen pics of me dressed - but this was the first time in person. They both took it well and her fiancé even gave me a kiss at the end of Auld Lang Syne!

The coming out to my mother just after Christmas was rather less agreeable. During the actual discussion, she seemed to accept my situation - but I subsequently learned that she had not taken it as well as I had thought. Her view is that she can only see me as her son and expects me to respect her position and not visit her en femme. I don't see this as a serious problem at the moment. I believe that she will eventually accept the inevitable - but she will need time to adjust. At least she is still talking to me and accepts my right to live my live as I must.

Anyway, I guess the overall score is pretty favourable. My daughter is the most important - and she has no problems with me as Helen. My mother's reaction was actually pretty much as I expected and I can live with her views. (At least she wasn't too upset with the news.

On the job front, it seems I have a pretty good chance of being taken on for longer contracts and, as all my colleagues know about me, it's a reasonably comfortable working environment.

OK - that brings the diary up to date as far as Christmas/ New Year.

Since then, there have been further developments - which you'll have to go to the next page to read :-).

January- February 1999

Work has had its ups and downs; overtime (which was critical to my financial situation) was totally curtailed in February - but has been reinstated since.

As readers of my diary will know, I took a course last year in counselling. I anticipate having to wait until September of this year to take the next level. Then I saw an advert in a local paper for the course at Salford College. I applied and was accepted.

I took the first opportunity to come out to other course members - this has led to some very good conversations and a lot of intelligent questions. We have a residential weekend in April - which I plan to spend as Helen. I've already explained to most of the group that I only attend the course in male mode as I go straight from work. I'm aware that I can hardly appear as Helen at the weekend then revert to male mode for the remainder of the course - so I shall have to make arrangements to change in future before getting to class. Unfortunately, the classes start at 5.30pm and I already have to leave work early to even get there for that time. Changing on the way will obviously take time - so I shall have to leave work even earlier.

Talking of work, as mentioned above, we had a severe cut-back on overtime about a month ago - since when it's crept back in. Other than that, nobody has expressed any problem with me due to my situation (apart from the supervisor being convinced that sooner or later I'll get over it!!!) As mentioned last issue, I anticipated hearing that my contract was being extended. I've since been moved up from no 4 in the workshop to no 3 - in theory making my position a bit more secure. As it happens, the following week was when the overtime was slashed and the planned recruitment of another engineer was put on hold - so I'm still low person on the totem pole!

What else has been happening?

Oh yes - Gilda's 50th birthday party.

Gilda as you probably know is my girlfriend. She met me as Helen and does not like to see me male - although she can accept it these days. I know that this will sound ironic for those of you whose partners can't stand your TGism - and I really do know how lucky I am to have found her.

I was challenged to make her 50th birthday party one to remember. She didn't want to know any of the plans - she wanted to be surprised. I just hoped I wouldn't disappoint her. Her actual birthday was on 7th Feb. - a Sunday.

I decided to make it an official Vanity Club UK weekend; with a meal in Metz on the Saturday evening - then ending up in Napoleons ready for midnight and the start of her birthday. As well as the VC UK members, I was given a list of special friends she hoped would attend - and, of course, there were all of our friends from the Village.

E-mails were sent out; phone calls were made; personal invitations issued around the village. As the date of the party approached, we had 20 booked for the meal and as many again planning to join us in Napoleons.

Of course, no birthday party is complete without a cake! I considered buying one - but, in the end, decided to make it myself.

I bought a couple of Swiss roll trays and a pile of chocolate sponge mixes. The plan was to make a base using several layers of two sponges side by side - then build a platform on top of this base with further layers of sponge. As the individual sponges didn't seem thick enough, I bought some oblong chocolate (Gilda loves chocolate) fudge brownies - which I used to build up the top platform (they were sandwiched between two layers of sponge). The layers of sponge were stuck together using........... chocolate spread (what else?). Naturally a smooth surface was required for the icing of the message on the top of the cake. I thought about using icing sugar (coloured black) but decided on - guess what - chocolate melted all over the cake.

I would estimate that the final cake probably contained at least a gigacalorie!

To decorate the cake, I stuck 50 candles around the ledge of the base (they only just fitted); on top of the cake I iced "Gilda's how old? - Never". On the very top was a Barbie doll. I trimmed its hair and coloured it red and used some nail varnish on its lips to match the lipstick Gilda (and I) normally wear when we go out together (we got fed up of our lipsticks clashing after a few kisses). I also made a very short black dress - typical of what Gilda likes to wear. The "piece de resistance" was the Zimmer frame- complete with "high heel shoes" - I made for the doll to rest against!

The meal in Metz was fabulous. Amongst the guests were all of the special girlfriends Gilda had wanted invited, some of whom had travelled up from London; Hugh - my oldest mate - and his wife Janet (Hugh got into the spirit of the event by painting his nails different colours).

Gilda ended up dancing on the table!

After the meal, we wandered around to Napoleons.

As we entered Naps., we saw Frann - a very dear friend of mine - which was a fabulous surprise as she had had a major hip operation three days earlier! I couldn't believe that she had made such an effort to get there for the party and it meant one hell of a lot to both of us to see her there.

Just before midnight, the birthday cake was brought in from the car where Julie had kept it during the evening. (Thanks again Julie!)

We had gone upstairs by then so, having been given the nod by Julie, I led Gilda down the stairs. All you could see was the glow from 50 candles! It was incredible. Gilda duly blew out the candles and the cake was quickly devoured!

Gilda's verdict on her party was that it had been fabulous! Thanks a million to all who attended.

Mothering Sunday

Two very special events occurred on Mothering Sunday.

The first was being given a "Someone like a Mother" card by Gilda's two daughters. That meant a lot to me. The two of them accept me as female. They discuss things in front of me which they wouldn't in front of men.

The second special event was when I called my own mother to wish her "Happy Mother's Day". We chatted for a while and, for reasons I won't go into, she made a comment about having two marvellous children. I remarked that we still caused her problems though. "Not really" was her reply; "Oh?" I queried. "No - I'm coming round and it's not really a problem for me now" was her answer. We were obviously referring to my TGism. She then started to ask about the colours I wear when I go out and how my flat is decorated. I don't doubt for one moment that she still finds it difficult, but she is certainly making an effort and appears to be coming to terms with it. This really made my day.

And, on that note, I think it's appropriate to close this episode of my diary.

March 1999

I've said in the past that I've considered myself to be borderline TV/TS. I've also stated in "What Makes Us TG" that I believe that the innate TG drive within us is suppressed by social conditioning and other external influences - factors I call the TG Brake.

I believe that it is the net effect of the TG Drive less the TG Brake which determines the level of TG activity required at any specific time to satisfy our need to express our femininity.

As the braking forces diminish- as they tend to do - the net TG drive becomes more powerful. In some cases, this results in someone starting to dress late in life; in others a TV who has been dressing for years may decide that this is no longer enough. In some, someone who has never even cross dressed before may decide that they are TS - perhaps going through a short period of transvestism or pseudo transvestism before reaching this conclusion. I have encountered girls who reflect all of these possibilities.

I have anticipated for some time that I might find myself in the position of needing to go further. My braking forces have been steadily eroded over the last couple of years. Some still remain:

- concern over employment (in spite of protection for TSs in the UK, there are always ways around the law).
- fear of the side effects of taking hormones
- fear of personality changes affecting a very special relationship with Gilda, (SHE only wants to see me as Helen but will the hormones affect my sexuality? Will I start to feel uncomfortable in a lesbian relationship? Will I decide I need a man instead?)
- fear of the pain of GRS
- fear, particularly of the effects of Androcur - I've seen several friends close to suicide due to its effects.
- fear of being caught up with peer pressure or on what one friend calls the TS escalator:

A T* says she might be a TS, and all the TS's say "Great, well done", and our heroine steps onto the bottom of the escalator. Then she sees Russell, and all the TS's say "Yippee, great news, you "passed" the test" and our TS stands still on the escalator. You get the picture ... eventually the date for the op is announced, and all the TS's say "Yippee, well done gal" and our T* can't step off the escalator now

I really am aware of peer pressure. Express doubts about what you are or lack of commitment and you are not really TS - just a TV playing at it (an accusation levelled at me last year).

I believe that the step I'm taking is so crucial that I will only continue as long as it feels right for me. So far, I've taken one step at a time - again, each felt right at the time.

I did not announce in advance that I was going to see Russell Reid because I wanted to avoid any possible pressure. I've been tempted to keep the news of my visit to myself for the same reasons.

But I know that many girls value my views and advice. They relate to my position and how I've handled coming out and facing what I am.

I can't live my life for them. But it is dishonest of me to pretend to be what I am not.

I've come out as TG to friends, family, colleagues at work and at college. Now that I have made the decision that I am TS, how can I hide that fact from my TG friends?

It just doesn't make sense!

So, my friends, I admit it:

I have failed to remain TV. Having to stay in limbo for the rest of my life is not an attractive option.

It may be that I shall find the road ahead much more difficult than staying as I was. In that case, I shall have to reconsider my decision.

I do not consider that I have "progressed" from being TV to being TS. I don't for one moment consider TSism to be a step up from being TV. I envy TVs who are content to express both sides of their personalities.

But, I have a poster on the wall in my toilet which reads:

"Face Your Fears. Live Your Dreams"

"Dreams" seems to imply wanting to be TS. I don't. I want to be able to live fully as a woman. I feel totally comfortable in that position. When dressed male - THEN I feel I'm playing a role I don't enjoy.

So, it's time to *"Face my Fears"*.

The Demonstration

I had just finished packing my suitcase as Jean, my wife, called that my breakfast was on the table. The aroma of the bacon and eggs met me as I walked down the stairs. Jean had already started on her bowl of All Bran as I sat down.

"What time do you expect to get to Cambridge then?" she asked me.

"All being well by about 10 - if I don't get held up too much on the M25."

"I should have left before then myself, so give me a call at Carol's tonight, will you?"

"Of course, darling," I replied, "and I'll see you on Friday".

I was leaving on my monthly tour of regional offices: Cambridge this afternoon, Leeds tomorrow, Manchester on Wednesday, Birmingham on Thursday, then Bristol on Friday. The business would take about four or five hours at each office and the drives between each was a couple of hours - so it was hardly a punishing schedule.

Jean was also going to be away for the week, visiting a friend in Wrexham for a "good old chinwag".

I headed out of Farnborough and joined the M3 and towards London and debated whether to go clockwise or anticlockwise around the M25. The former involved the roadworks and the M4, M40 and M1 traffic; the alternative could involve delays at the Dartford crossing. Otherwise there really wasn't much in it with the M11 virtually diagonally opposite the M3. The choice between a potential few miles of congestion at the crossing or the certainty of heavy slow-moving traffic for most of the way around the M25 was settled in favour of Dartford.

A little over an hour later, I was emerged from the tunnel into Essex, well on time and, hopefully with the worst of the trip behind me. Now it should be a reasonably clear drive round to and up the M11. Then a couple of miles along the A45 - sorry, it's now the A14, to the Science Park on the northern outskirts of Cambridge.

The company I'd founded ten years earlier had a modern unit which we used for our computer training courses. These ranged from basic introductions to computing through to advanced techniques for spreadsheets, databases, graphics programmes and the like. The basic courses were fairly routine - except when Microsoft launch a new version of Windows such as Windows 95 and all our material had to be updated; the advanced courses were a different matter. Every time a package was updated, we had to assess the new facilities provided and modify our courses to suit. The biggest problems were always filling the available spaces and, if we achieved that target, deciding whether to increase the number of places we could offer and assessing whether or not to provide a new course on a specialist subject.

If the part of the journey I least enjoyed was the run around London on the M25, then the highlight was the Wednesday evening in Manchester where I would be able to get along to the Concord meeting.

This trip, I was conscious that Jean would only be about an hour's drive from Manchester and that I could have met up with her at Carol's - but, fortunately, she had specifically instructed me not to.

"This is a girls' week - no men at all." I had been told quite firmly. "Peter is off to Dusseldorf for an exhibition so Carol and I are going to do nothing but natter."

It struck me as vaguely ironic that I would probably be doing exactly the same thing that Wednesday - catching up on gossip with the other girls! The main difference being that Carol and Jean would probably be slouching around in jeans and sweaters without any make-up while I would be dressed in a frock and would have spent ages in front of the mirror getting my face on. Doubly ironic, in fact considering that both of them were

"Image Consultants" specialising on the colours women (and men) should wear to suit their own complexions, hair etc.

It was one of my main regrets that I had been unable to tell Jean about my transvestism, but I had never dared doing so because I didn't want to risk losing her. We had recently celebrated our silver wedding and our children had left home. During the past twenty-five years, I had been through the usual phases of thinking that I could give up being a tv - indeed, had done so for several years when we wed. More recently, I had come to terms with the reality that it was incurable and, just as important, harmless. Jean had never been deprived of anything as a result of my transvestism and it gave me an escape from the stresses of running a successful business.

I realised, however, that not everyone has a TVs view of cross dressing and that a high proportion of the public considered it perverted. I was also aware that it could cause business problems if my secret was ever revealed.

To avoid such a risk, I took a number of precautions when I visited Manchester. I had a small flat, not far from the city centre, which nobody knew about, where I kept "Katherine's" clothes. I would drive to the hotel where I was officially registered, check in, then take a taxi to the flat; change then take another taxi to the Rem.

This Wednesday, I got to the village at about 6.30 so had a meal in Boodles before going to the Rem.

When I arrived, discovered that there was a make-up and colour co-ordination demonstration that evening, carried over from the previous week. I had often thought that this would be an ideal subject for the group. Jean had, of course, advised me on colours for clothes - but this took account of my natural greying hair rather than the auburn wig I usually wore.

I bought a drink from the bar then joined Faye, Jackie and Gwen and catch up on the news.

Half an hour later, Mary announced that the presentation was about to start. I'd had my back to the door, so hadn't even seen the demonstrators arrive.

"Good evening, ladies. As you know, this presentation was planned for last week. Unfortunately, I was involved in a minor accident and was unable to get here in time. As it happens, the delay has probably been providential as two of my colleagues have agreed to help me out this evening. I'll introduce them to you in a few moments," announced the consultant.

"I have to tell you that this booking had me worried. I had no idea what to expect. In fact, to be honest, it was probably that which distracted me last week and resulted in the accident. I told a colleague of mine about my concerns and she agreed to give me some moral support, she also had a friend of hers staying who is also one of our consultants and who is also here. I have to say, however, that, having met a couple of you and your wives for a meal last night, my concerns were totally groundless. In fact, my colleagues aren't here to provide moral support any longer - but because we were all fascinated and impressed with what we learned yesterday. We were particularly interested to hear that some estimates say that 50 percent of men dress up, which means that one and a half of our husbands is probably a tv, well say at least one could well be! And if they aren't, we will just have to convert them, won't we?"

"Right, first the introductions. I'm Linda. My area covers Manchester and I'll be only too happy to arrange personal consultations for any of you. This is Carol from Wrexham and Jean from Farnborough in Hampshire."

Fair Cop

Yes Officer - 1

I had been out for a drive dressed, done a bit of shopping, had a coffee - and it was now time to get changed and head for home. It was just getting dark and I found a secluded area just off a country side road. I was wearing a long raincoat so undid my button through skirt and was pulling on my trousers when a police motorcyclist rode past; I heard him turn round and he drove over to me.

"Good evening, sir. What are you doing here?" he asked.

"Just having a rest" I replied

"I see, is this your car? Have you got any identification?"

I handed him my driving license while he checked out my car registration and got confirmation of the registered keeper.

"You seem nervous sir" he commented.

I explained that I was getting changed.

"I see. Well, there is nothing illegal in what you say you are doing - but there have been some thefts from the sailing club across the road. If there hasn't been anything taken tonight there will be nothing to worry about but if there has been a theft we will know where to find you."

There hadn't been - so that was the end of the matter.

Yes Officer - 2

Driving home from a Northern Concord Meeting I noticed a police van behind me. Was he following me? Had I been exceeding the speed limit? The answer to the former was yes - and I couldn't be entirely certain that I hadn't been speeding. Oh sh*t.

He pulled me over and a policeman accompanied by a policewoman approached me.

"Are you Mr XXX?" he asked. They had obviously already checked out my registration.

"Yes" I replied.

"Nothing to worry about - just a routine check - would you come back to the van with us?"

As I got out of the car and walked to the van, he said that the reason I'd been stopped was because of a faulty brake light. I said that I could hardly check that while driving. (I suspect they were checking for drink driving)

"No that's OK, I'll just give you a form to get signed when you've had it repaired then you take it along to your local station and that will be the end of the matter" he said.

As he was filling in the form, he had to keep referring to codes for various boxes.

"I don't usually bother with these, I usually just book people" he told me.

There was obviously an advantage in being in a skirt!

"Been out for the evening, have you?" he asked "what do you think of Manchester?"

"I think it's great - I can dress as I want and no-one cares"

They both laughed.

Don't you just love our policemen and women?

The Dream

For those of us whose families are, as far as we are aware, ignorant of our transvestism, I'm quite certain that being able to share our secret and have it accepted is a dream; whilst being found out and being rejected as a consequence is a perennial nightmare.

The first instance that I can recall dressing must have been when I was about nine years old, it was my sister's best pink party frock. Since then, like so many TVs, I've "given up" for periods only to have something trivial trigger the need.

I was going through one of my suppression phases when I met my wife. This lasted throughout the three years of our engagement while I studied at evening classes for my professional exams and even the first year of our marriage. I stopped again six years later when our daughter was born - only to start again when I had to visit Newcastle on business and spotted a pair of size 10 high heels in a Lilley & Skinner sale. Across the road from the shopping centre was a dress shop selling larger sizes which had quite an attractive dress in the window.

"If", I thought, "if I was to start dressing again, what would I need and how much would it cost? How much could I afford to charge to Access and Barclaycard? Could I get everything I'd need? I've seen some shoes and a dress. The wig. That's the critical item. I'll bet there isn't anywhere locally I could get a wig - and, if there is, I'll bet the total cost of everything would be more than I can afford to spend." I found a coffee shop and made a quick list: dress, shoes, wig, tights, panties, bra, handbag, make up & cleansers, purse. Then I went round the shops and priced everything. So, £60 or so for everything except the wig. Let's say I can afford £100 - that leaves about £40 for the wig. IF I can find a wig for under £40, I'll do it!" I must have found a wig because I started again.

My job at this time gave me plenty of opportunities for dressing with business trips around the country. Then disaster struck. I lost my job and with it the opportunity to dress. Perhaps it was a punishment! I packed up all of my feminine apparel and dumped it. I can and will beat this disease! I thought.

That was in 1984. Six years later, we had a competition in our village and, as we were expected to dress up for the final's night, the wife of one of the other members of the team I was in suggested that we should dress as women. I put up a nominal resistance to the idea - but finally agreed to do it if the others did.

Most of the clothes could probably be found for us but I knew that none of the wives took my size in shoes and I also knew I would have serious difficulty finding any in our local town. So the next week, I headed for the nearest Saxones. A suitable pair of shoes was located and purchased. At least I would be ready if the scheme went ahead.

As it happens, one of the other members of the team flatly refused to dress up. So the opportunity to let my wife and daughter see me dressed and, maybe, develop the subject, was lost.

Needless to say, the shoes were soon followed by other items and it wasn't long before I was dressing completely again. As both my wife and daughter had been very keen to see me dressed as a woman, it is possible that they would accept my transvestism. But there is a very big difference between dressing up for a laugh and being a tv.

By 1994, my business was in dire straits with mounting debts and I took on some temping work during the summer to supplement my other work. This assignment lasted rather longer than the anticipated 2-3 weeks and led to me being offered a contract on the next project in North Wales - an hour away from Manchester. I jumped at the opportunity. It would, of course, involve me living away from home and, in order to maximise overtime earnings, would prevent me from getting home very often. My wife was happy that the money was excellent and would help us to start clearing off some of our debts.

I'm currently living in a caravan. My wife still lives in our house in Cambridgeshire and our daughter is at university. This means that I am free to dress when I wish. I can get over to Concord meetings virtually every Wednesday as well as spending most Saturday evenings in the Village.

That, at least, is how it was until the Mayday bank holiday weekend.

As usual, I had planned to take advantage of the volume of work to do some heavy overtime over the weekend and on the Monday. I started at 6.30am on the Saturday morning and finished at about 3. I had spoken to my wife on the phone during the morning and checked that there were no problems at home. Back at the caravan, I sorted out my clothes for the evening and, after a few chores, went for a shower. By just before 6 I was ready to leave. I'd done most of my make-up and had pulled a pair of trousers and a jacket over my dress. My shoes, wig and handbag were in a case in the car ready for the next stage of my transition. Sunglasses hid my made-up eyes and I would take my chances that nobody would be close enough to notice that my face was powdered.

A few miles down the road, I pulled into a layby, pulled on my wig, applied lipstick, removed my trousers and change out of the trainers I'd been wearing into a pair of low-heeled shoes for driving. I put on my jewellery and applied my false nails. Fifteen minutes later I was back on the road and heading for Manchester.

I had my usual (excellent) meal in the Blue Café and walked round to Paddy's Goose. It was a relatively quiet evening with a number of regulars missing, but still a pleasant evening. I decided against going on to Napoleons and headed back to my caravan - stopping en route to slip my trousers back over my dress, and remove my wig and make up.

Being a holiday weekend, the site was relatively full and it was not until I was actually at my caravan that I noticed an unexpected Mini parked there. It was my wife's. The door to the van opened and she stepped out and came across to me.

"I think you've got some explaining to do" she said, holding up the make-up bag I'd left out earlier.

I followed her into the caravan and closed the door behind me.

"So, where is she? Don't try and deny it, I can even smell her perfume on you!". She demanded. "Had an argument have you - she obviously spends nights here because her nightie is on the bed."

"It's not what you think." I replied. "Mind you, you might prefer your original assumption to have been correct".

"What do you mean?"

"You've found some make-up and stuff and assume that I'm having an affair."

"Well - what other explanation is there? And don't say that you lent the caravan to a friend for a bit of the other, because I won't believe you!"

"I think you'd better sit down". I told her. I took a deep breath.

"I'm not having an affair" I continued, "the items you've found are mine. I'm a transvestite. That's someone who...... "

"I know what a transvestite is." she said in a calmer voice. "I assume you've been out dressed this evening. So where do you go? And what do you get up to? Do you go with men? Are you planning to have an operation? God, what a mess".

"Yes, I've been out dressed this evening. I went over to Manchester, had a meal and met up with some friends. I'm not gay - although the transvestite scene is in the gay village in Manchester and we do mix with gays and straights. And no, I'm not planning to have the op."

"I think I need a drink." she said. "What have you got?"

"Only tea or coffee, I'm afraid".

"Coffee will have to do then".

As I filled the kettle and put it to boil, the questions continued.

"How long have you been a transvestite?"

"Why couldn't you tell me about it?"

"How much have you spent on it?"

"What makes you do it?"

I answered her as far as I could.

"Have you got any photographs of yourself?"

I found the pictures taken at recent Concord events in copies of Cross Talk and passed them to her. I also found some photographs taken in Paddy's Goose.

"This is you? I don't believe it! You actually look very attractive." She then turned to those taken in Paddy's. "You're not going to tell me that all of these are transvestites. And who are these women with their arms around you?"

"Those two are just friends - and I mean just friends." I gave her a coffee.

"Aren't you hot in that jacket" she asked. "Oh God. Don't tell me, you're still dressed underneath, aren't you? Well, come on; let's see you in the flesh."

I went out to the car and collected my wig, handbag and high heels.

I picked up the make-up bag from where Joan had tossed it and did my face.

As she watched me, Joan became astounded. "You really are good at that. It takes me far longer. No wonder you kept moaning at me to hurry up when we go out."

I took out my earrings, slipped them through my lobes and secured them with the butterfly clasps.

"When did you have your ears pierced?" she asked.

Next I shook out my wig and pulled and brushed it into place. Finally, I took off the jacket and trousers and let my dress fall into place before slipping on my high heels.

"I don't know what to say", she remarked. "When I first found the evidence, I was convinced you were having an affair. In fact, I was about to leave when you came back. Then, when you told me that you were a transvestite, I had visions of you looking absolutely dreadful, until I saw the photographs and even then, I couldn't believe it. But you look great. I also noticed that you look far more relaxed dressed that I've seen you in a long time." she continued. "I'm not saying that I'm not hurt that you didn't let me know before although I can understand why you didn't."

"So, where do we go from here?" I asked her.

"I'm going to have to come with you and meet some of your friends, they seem to be having a lot more fun than I do down in Cambridgeshire - and I'm not leaving you alone with those two "friends" of yours. I'm obviously not going to be able to stop you dressing so I'd better learn to live with it. It may not be easy and I'm sure there'll be problems, but nothing we can't overcome. Now come here, you can help me live out one of my fantasies while you're dressed like that!"

It was a dream come true!

Then the alarm went off!

Can You Tell Me What I Am?

Can you tell me what I am?
Neither woman nor a man
Not a sister, nor a brother
Not a father, not a mother

I can no longer live as a male
Yet can I be a "real" female
Am I to be trapped in the middle?
Is there an answer to this riddle?

Living as I simply have to be
A woman is what I hope people see
Yet when others, of me, do speak,
Do they see me as a freak?

For fifty years, my mother's son was I,
But between my legs there was a lie.
For fifty years I lived my life
Battling with internal strife

As a boy child I was taught that I
should be strong and never cry
To be a rock and solid foundation
To be a credit to our nation

Men have to fight and try to win,
To strive for success, and not give in
Women could their emotions show
But tears I could ne'er allow to flow

When my father died, I had to keep
A "stiff upper lip" and not to weep
A small sob was all that I did spare
But did this mean I couldn't care?
Through most of this time I felt stress
from a feminine side I must suppress
From time to time 'she' would emerge
When I couldn't resist that dreadful urge

The effect of that struggle within me deep
Made me cause others to hurt and to weep
I know I caused others pain and stress
How I wish I'd hurt them less.

I had to leave home to work to live
This, a new chance to me did give
to find myself and what I could be
Now I need not deny the real me

I found new friends who would accept me
for who I was and not how I *ought* to be
Helen was now allowed to live
Because of the love they did give

One became much more than a friend,
Beside her, my life I wanted to spend
Her love showed that I could be
accepted as the real me

I wasn't looking for love when I found her,
I was happy to be her friend and nothing more.
Then, as our friendship, into love, grew
happiness, like never before, I knew.

Her acceptance meant the world to me.
At last, I could be who I *should* be.
The guilt and shame I'd felt in the past
was overcome by her love at last

She gave me love, She gave me joy,
There's so very much we did enjoy.
She gave me hope, She gave me life,
She took away so much strife.

When I struggled o'er where my future lay
she was there for me every single day
and when, sometimes, things went wrong
her true love helped me stay strong

Without her there as things got tough
I may have said "enough's enough"
but her love gave me the strength
to face the road whate'er its length

When cruel insults at me were thrown
her love stopped me from feeling down.
When I faltered, my hand she'd hold
and in holding me, she'd make me bold.

Without her love and her unfailing support
those vicious taunts much more would hurt
Was it destiny, was it the fates,
that made us such true soulmates?

As the date approaches for surgery
I pray she'll still be there for me
I face some times of doubts and fear.
To get me through, I need her near.

My emotions are surely bound to be
up and down and I need to see
her there to carry me through.
Without her what will I do?

She was there when I needed her
to conquer my doubts and my fear.
To accept me for who I am.
To believe in me and tell me I can.

Without her love and support, perhaps I
would not have had the courage to try.
Her love helped find the strength to be
the woman I am; to be the real me.

But now I no longer sleep at her side
Because she finds I cannot provide
Something she needs to her own self to be true
Being without her there makes me so blue

She only sees me as a woman she says
Yet a female body for love she desires
Even the operation may not the answer be
to let her be satisfied with me

If I cannot give that which she does crave
I must face my loss and with it the grave
of the love of which we did sing
As I am left with nothing

Does the problem lie with me?
Does she in me a male still see?
If **even she** still sees me as male
How can I ever be truly female?

Fifty years I spent learning how
to be seen to be male and I must now
over fewer weeks than those long years
change how I'm seen - else face the tears.

Other friends say they only see the "she"
Then, from nowhere, they call me "he"
Slips such as these, doubts must raise
about how others do me perceive

Where does all this now leave me?
If partly male they still me see?
Am I neither woman nor man?
Can you tell me what I am?

If she who really cared cannot me see
as truly female - can there be hope for me?
In spite of all I try and all I seek
Must I remain a total freak?

Is there any point in struggling on
now my dreams may have all gone?
Was I fooling myself to think I can
ever be accepted as a real woman?

<snip>

The surgeons' work now is done
And a new life for me has begun
Nearly three years have now passed
A friendship replaced the love I lost

My body has changed and so have my needs
To a different attraction I now concede
But my past still retains
It's ability to cause me pain

Guys seem interested in me
'til they learn my history
When they learn how I was born,
They leave me and I'm forlorn.

Jokes are made of men who with us have sex
They highlight a problem which does us vex
Do we tell of our past and, if so, when?

Do we risk the loss of love, yet again?

Can you tell me what I am?
Neither woman nor a man
Not a sister, nor a brother
Not a father, not a mother

Coming Out 1 — Mission Impossible

On Sunday 29th March 1998, two of my oldest male mates - Hugh & Mike - phoned me to say they were planning to pay me a surprise visit the following Saturday. I warned them that they would have a shock if they did arrive without warning. "They didn't know what I get up to up here" I warned them. "That was the idea, to catch you at it" said Mike (the other mate). We had a lot of banter about this for half an hour. They were sure I was winding them up. I encouraged them to think that this was the case.

I have always been concerned that one (Hugh) would turn up unexpectedly. He has done so plenty of times in the past when I was living in Cambridgeshire - phoning from his mobile and saying "put the coffee on I'll be there in 5 minutes". If he were to do so now, he would be confronted with Helen.

Rather than risk a confrontation, I'd prefer to introduce the subject in a controlled manner.

We are supposed to be meeting at Stoke on Trent next Sat (11th April). Hugh wants to visit a big motorcycle dealer there. They then plan to stay at the flat Sat night.

I have prepared a series of four "briefing papers" for them.

This is in 4 stages. If their response to any stage is negative; then I walk away and say that they can never visit the flat - but that I will meet them at another venue should they come to Manchester.

Up to the final revelation; they will almost certainly think I am still winding them up. They'll be able to walk away and not be sure that I do have a secret.

I shall attempt to retain this impression.

As you'll see, the last stage before the revelation is a form with a list of possible activities - some sexually based, some anorakish, some the truth. They'll believe that I could be involved in the anorakish ones (eg American line dancing, 60's music, model making/ radio-controlled yachts etc) as I've done similar things in the past. I don't think they'll believe that it's bondage/S&M etc. I expect them to say they can't handle some of the anorakish activities - but that they'll go along with the gag on most of the others.

IF they say they can't handle the "cross dressing" & "Gay Village" activities. Then I'll just say "sorry guys, you've said you can't handle what I do - so I guess there's no option but for us to go our separate ways and for you to avoid my flat permanently"

If they don't tick those boxes, I give them the final revelation sheets. I expect them to still think I'm kidding until they see the photograph that's printed on the second of the pages.

So, next Saturday could be interesting.

It could back fire on me. They may not tick the cd & village boxes thinking it's still a gag. They may still not be able to accept this. Oh well - then I'll blame them.

I could be about to lose two of my oldest male mates. But I don't see that I have any choice. Better to do it this way (I think) than to simply say "don't come and see me" or risking them just turning up on the doorstep one day and coming face to face with Helen.

One thing I am reasonably certain of is that they'll keep my secret. I hope so. Mind you I may be about to find out that they already know - and, perhaps, that my wife does as well.

There was one incident many years ago when I walked into our dining room to find Hugh saying something about transvestism to my wife. I didn't hear very much but what I did hear was accurate. I'm pretty certain Hugh will be OK with it. Not quite so sure about Mike. As Hugh has a full beard/ moustache, it's not likely that he is TV himself.

Call back after next Saturday to find out what happened.

The "Briefing Papers"

As stated, Hugh & Mike probably think I am kidding about the "secret activities" that I get up to. We frequently wind each other up. So far, I suspect that they think I am joking. I plan to keep up the impression that this is the situation until the final revelation.

That way if there is any negative feedback, I can walk away and just say "OK guys, you can't accept what I do - so if you ever come to Manchester, I guess we'll have to meet somewhere other than the flat (apartment to those across the pond)".

The actual paper to be given to them follows, some of you may be old enough to have seen the television series "Mission Impossible". If I had a small portable tape player, I'd probably have presented it THAT way:

Preliminary briefing notes

Preamble

Your jointly declared intention of penetrating the security zone hitherto known as Mike's Manchester Mess (MMM) has made it necessary to expose some, if not all, of the activities based therein.

It has been deemed far safer to your mental well-being to expose these activities in a controlled manner rather than risk a surprise visit and immediate unprepared confrontation.

The revelations required by this may or may not be significant. Nevertheless, any information revealed must be held in the strictest possible confidence regardless of whether or not you accept the challenge of visiting MMM and proceeding with this evening's mission whatever that might or might not entail.

The security classification is "Eyes Only". No information may be revealed about the activities in and around MMM and any other locations visited as part of the mission to any other person whatsoever. This specifically includes all who may have contact with any members of the family or in-laws of any participants in the activities.

You are free to withdraw from the mission at any time.

No photographs may be taken during the mission.

No sound or video recordings may be made during the mission.

No attempt may be made to identify others who may be encountered during the mission.

If, and only if, you are prepared to accept these conditions, sign this form. You will then proceed to briefing stage two.

Stage 2 Briefing Notes — Mission Limitations

The Mission is to accompany me to MMM and other locations. You may participate in the activities or act as observers as you choose.

The conditions in MMM would inevitably have revealed the nature of the activities which take place there and in other locations to be visited as part of the mission.

It would have taken substantial time and effort to have sanitised MMM for a visit to eliminate the risk of exposure of the activities based therein.

Even if MMM had been sanitised, it is likely that contacts made by others involved in the activities which occur at MMM would have resulted in my own "cover" being blown.

For this reason, I have decided that I have no option but to give you the choice of learning of those activities and keeping them totally secret - or seeking an assurance from you never to attempt to penetrate the MMM security zone at any time.

The activities are NOT illegal. Some may, however, consider them subversive.

They will almost certainly make you reconsider your opinion of me.

The planned activities will not expose you to any physical risks other than those normally involved in a major city such as Manchester. I can offer no such assurances concerning your mental well-being.

It should be made clear that I have valued your friendships for some 35 years.

I do not wish to lose that friendship. I will, nevertheless, understand if you feel unable to contact me again in future should you proceed to stage 3 and learn of my activities.

Do you wish to continue?

Should your decision be positive, you may still withdraw from the mission at any time. But this is the last opportunity to do so without being exposed to the truth.

If your answer is NO, you should leave immediately.

You can then retain your current opinion of me and believe that I have been "winding you up" - which could be the truth of course.

Briefing Notes — The Secret?

So what is the secret?

What "subversive" activities take place within the security zone at MMM?

Listed below are some possibilities. Consider them. One or more are true. Are there any you could not handle?

Subject	I can believe this	Sorry, but if this is true, I couldn't handle it
Girlfriend(s)		
Orgies		
Bondage Parties		
S&M		
Cross-dressing		
Nightclubbing		
Gay Village		
Folk Club		
60's music club		
American line dancing		
Wine making/ tasting group		
Model making club		
Scale model racing		
Radio controlled yachts		
Radio controlled aircraft		
Amateur Radio		

Warning.

If any of the subjects ticked as "can't handle" are correct, then I shall have to ask you never to penetrate the security zone around MMM.

Should you NOT tick any box as "can't handle", you will be expected to participate in the evening's activities - even if only as an observer. Think VERY carefully about your answers.

If neither of them tick "cross dressing/ gay village as "can't handle" - then they get the following. (What happens if one does and the other doesn't? Good question. I don't know) I guess I tell them that one has ticked a box that indicates that he can't handle my activities so in fairness they should go.

Stage 4 — The Revelation

No, it's not a joke guys. I do have a secret that I've kept for 40 odd years.

Or, at least, I believe it's a secret - maybe you already know somehow.

I am a transvestite.

I visit tranny friendly venues in Manchester's gay village at least a couple of times a week. In fact, I am probably one of the best-known TVs on the Manchester scene and on the Internet. I am involved in support groups and am President of a major Internet based tranny club - Vanity Club UK.

I have been involved in helping dozens of trannies to accept that their condition is not a perversion - but an inherent medical condition which is caused pre-natally.

My flat is well known as a haven for trannies. It's far from unusual for a dozen or so to visit it at different times each week. This will include transvestites and transsexuals. When I said there were half a dozen girls around most weekends, I wasn't kidding - though perhaps not the sort of girls you'd fancy.

I am not gay - but have quite a few gay friends through mixing with them.

I didn't ask to be a TV. But as I am - I now enjoy it after years of guilt and shame.

Since my contract ended at Christmas, I've spent nearly all of my time living in female role other than when it's necessary to dress in male mode - signing on etc.

All of the income I've generated since Christmas has been from tranny contacts. The computer course last weekend was for trannies. They give TVs an excuse to come to Manchester - which has the best TV scene in the UK (probably the world). You wondered why I wasn't devastated to be offered a job in Manchester Hugh - and why I stayed on here when the contract ended? Now you know.

No-one has a definitive answer about the cause of transvestism - but if you are a transvestite, it is an integral part of your nature and cannot be ignored. Try to fight it and it creates stress. I've stopped dressing several times in the past - for up to 6 years at a stretch. But it re-emerges eventually. I've now stopped trying to stop - and have come to terms with what I am.

It was during one of my denial periods that I met and married Jenny. I've fought it in the past; I've been totally ashamed of it and felt guilty as hell over it. I don't any longer - but I still have no wish to risk upsetting Jenny, Joanna or my mother if they were to find out as I am not sure that they could understand it.

I ask, therefore that you respect my request not to tell anyone. I would not have risked telling either of you if I thought I could not trust you.

I appreciate that this revelation may be difficult to come to terms with. If you prefer not to come to the flat, I'll understand - though I hope you will and give me a chance to answer any questions you may have.

This evening

I would normally go out to the pubs and clubs in the Village on a Saturday evening. I'd like you to join me.

You may not feel comfortable with this idea. But I can assure you that whilst you will see some very strange sights, you will not be at any risk and you will have a very interesting evening. It will certainly be educational and I think you'll be at your ease fairly quickly.

Most of my TV friends are well presented - forget any idea of a load of Kenny Everett or Dame Edna Everage look alikes. (Though there are one or two around). TVs come from virtually every background. The conversation is not a lot different to other groups of friends getting together - perhaps with rather less emphasis on football.

You may find it strange hearing TVs calling each other by their femme names - and seeing me dressed as "Helen".

Well, it's up to you. Now you know my darkest secret. I hope it won't affect our friendship.

Ask what you like and I'll try to answer the questions as far as I can.

Well, that's it. That's how I propose to handle my coming out to a couple of old friends.

There was then a photo of me and some friends dressed en femme

Without the picture - they'd probably still believe that I am winding them up. That SHOULD show them that I am not joking.

I may yet chicken out. But I intend leaving the flat as it is - and THAT would expose matters so unless I say sorry guys you still can't come to the flat, I'm going to force myself to go through with the revelation. Chances are that even if I was to clear it up and hide all my femme gear, I'd overlook something. I'd almost certainly get half a dozen phone calls during the time they were there. They'd probably want to use my PC to get onto the internet and I'd have to hide all my bookmarks.

In any case, as I've already said, Hugh IS likely to turn up unexpectedly sometime. At least this way I stand a better chance of him accepting things than if he was to just be confronted by Helen.

There is, of course, another scenario:

They may already be aware of what I am and do.

It's even possible that they are aware that I am Helen - and are regular visitors to my pages. Are you? If so, maybe I'll be confronted with the forms already filled in when we meet up!

Wish me luck.

Well, I did it.

We met in Stoke on Trent; visited a very large motorcycle dealership - which was the other reason Hugh wanted to come up this way, then went for a drink and some lunch in a pub.

I passed them the various stages of the revelation documents - as expected, they thought I was still winding them up. The only "can't handle" as far as possible activities were concerned was "American Line Dancing" from Mike.

As I passed them the last envelope, I took a heck of a deep breath and said "I'm really not sure whether I should let you have this"; Hugh said "well, it's your decision". "Read it" I said - then watched his face. His eyes widened as he read the statement that I was a TV.

When they'd both read them, I asked "well?".

"Makes no difference" was the answer I got from both of them. "Why should it?" They asked

Pushing my luck, I asked how they felt about the planned evening in the village with Helen. "No problem"

We then went back to my flat, played a game of cards - then I announced that it was time for me to have a bath and get changed for the evening.

Even when I returned to the lounge dressed, there was just total acceptance of Helen. By the end of the evening, they were both calling me Helen (with occasional lapses through force of habit).

I could not have dared hope for a better response - or evening with them.

We went to Metz for a meal; then into Paddy's Goose, Dotz, Cafe Hollywood, Napoleons - then back to the flat with some of the other girls: Julie, Jane, Jacqui, Jackie, Susan, Kath; Sal & Martin also came back with us.

Mike was a bit reserved at times - but still had no problem chatting to some of the others. Hugh simply took it in his stride and thoroughly enjoyed himself.

There was an initial shock when they read the "revelation" - and at that point I think both were convinced that it was still a "wind-up". As they continued to read the final pages, they realised that I was totally serious - but it has made no difference.

Neither of them had had any idea that I am TV. Hugh can't recall the conversation he had with my wife - so it obviously didn't relate to me - which eliminates the one possible question mark I'd had about my wife knowing about my transvestism. Now I am 100% certain that she doesn't.

Well, what else can I say. It went brilliantly.

I should be feeling over the moon - and I guess I do feel very very relieved. I'm also drained after the tension of the last week and knackered after a late night.

Coming Out 2 — At Work

In 1998, I was working in a computer workshop. I'd originally been told that the placement was open ended — but, when I started there, I was told it was only for a couple of weeks. The workshop supervisor was Iranian and to say he was homophobic is like suggesting Hitler disliked Jews.

One morning - about 3 weeks after I started there, he asked me if I'd seen a programme on Channel 4 the previous night with drag queens and their partners. His views were somewhat extreme. (Put the lot of them against a wall and shoot them). I tried to explain that most trannies are not gay - but he wouldn't accept this. "They must be to dress as women". "They also need treatment - a pill or injection or something to cure them". Again, I tried to explain that transvestism is not an illness and can't be cured.

It was like talking to a brick wall.

So, I asked him how many TVs he knew. He stepped back in horror at the thought of knowing any, threw his hands in the air and shook his head.

"Well, I'm one" I told him.

"What do you mean?" he asked.

"I am a transvestite. When I'm not working, I dress as a woman. That's why I know about the subject."

"I need a cigarette" he said, visibly shocked, and went outside. (I wanted one too - but thought it wiser to keep out of his way for a while).

"Sh*t" I thought, sitting at my bench. "That's the job down the pan".

I hadn't just lost my cool with him - I had deliberately decided to take a stand with him and show him that his views were wrong. I could NOT stand by any longer and listen to utter crap from people who are totally ignorant of our condition. As there was every likelihood that my contract would end on Friday anyway, I'd taken the view that I hadn't got too much to lose in any case. Even so, I wondered if he'd ask me to leave immediately in view of his opinions and maybe even complain to the agency.

He subsequently came up to me and said whilst he didn't understand what I am, he respected my work and me as a person and offered to make me a coffee. Later that day he was trying to extend my assignment.

The assignment was still extended - in fact at the time of writing (early November) it looks like it will last at least until the end of the year and probably well into 1999 with luck!

Since the revelation, the topic has come up several times. On one occasion, I was thinking that I wished he wouldn't keep speaking about it as I really didn't want it to get around the workshop. When I turned round and saw the other engineers gathered in a semi-circle listening, I realised that everyone now knew that I am TG - and seriously considering going further. They even asked to see photographs and were quite complimentary. There has, so far, been absolutely no negative reaction - other than the supervisor's lack of understanding and his view that I could and, perhaps, should "cure" myself through determination!

Coming Out 3 — to Jo and Jenny

I'd already told Jo and Jenny about my trip to the Rocky Horror Picture Show and they'd demanded to see the photographs. When I went to see them at Jenny's House in August 98, I was hardly through the door before my daughter pounced.

"Have you got them with you?" she asked.

"Yes" I replied.

"Let's see them then" she demanded.

I suggested that they should go into the lounge and sit down to look at them.

The photographs were greeted with peals of laughter - while I looked on.

"You think it's funny me being dressed as a woman?" I asked quietly.

"Of course," was the response.

I took a deep breath. "I do it all the time" I said, "I'm a transvestite, here are some other photos of me".

"What?" asked my wife. I repeated what I had just said.

Jo just said "cool".

There was a longish question and answer session covering the usual topics:

How long had I been TV? - all my life - though it had been during a purge stage that we had met and married.

How had I hidden everything? - in the garage.

Am I going to have the op? - maybe - I don't know at the moment what will happen

Am I gay? - I don't fancy men, but have no idea how I will feel in the future due to the effects of hormones if I decide to go further. At the moment I'd probably turn out to be a lesbian.

Why hadn't I said anything earlier? Because I didn't understand it myself and could not expect her to accept something I felt disgusted about. By the time I realised it was nothing to be ashamed of, I was living away and I felt it was best to wait until our daughter had finished her degree. (Which my daughter thanked me for).

Is being TV why you don't want to move back here? Yes. I would not expect you to put up with me dressing around the house and wanting to go in and out as a woman. (She agreed this would not have been acceptable).

I also pointed out that we had effectively agreed to separate the last time I had been "home". She said that she had planned to raise the subject that weekend as well.

We agreed that there was no "blame" to be attached to the marriage ending. We both felt our interests had drifted apart and that there was no point in pretending otherwise. We discussed splitting the property. I said I didn't want anything from her home other than personal items; I would keep what I had in Manchester and we agreed that there would be no ongoing financial commitments between us.

All in all, a very amicable settlement of the situation.

They both wished me luck in the future as "Helen" whatever that involves.

Read it and Weep

When I went to see Russell Reid about being transsexual, he provided a letter that I could take to my GP.

When I received the letter, I met up with a couple of transsexual friends in Churchill's bar in the village. When I arrived, they were deep in conversation about hormones.

"Can anyone join in?" I asked.

"Sorry, it's girl talk" Kym said – meaning "we" are transsexual, "you" are transvestite. (There was no malice in this it was just a bit of banter).

"Read it and weep" I told them – passing over Russell's letter.

She only had to see the headed notepaper to know what it would say.

"About time!" said Kym. "You kept quiet about going to see him, didn't you?"

So don't believe me!

It's amazing that you can tell people you cross-dress and they think you are joking!

The Handbag

I was shopping in a supermarket when I saw a white handbag which was perfect to go with some 3" court shoes I'd got.

At the checkout I was packing my groceries into a carrier bag when the girl said "I'd better put this handbag in a carrier for you as well - don't want people wondering what a man is doing with a handbag"

"It goes with my white high heels" I told her.

She laughed.

I was tempted to go back there dressed and prove I hadn't been joking!

The Posters

My work involved computer support and I had CorelDraw on my pc which was ideal for producing posters. I had done one for near the coffee making facility with a picture of a maid and the message "we haven't got a maid - so clear up after yourself".

Someone else wanted one for a golf tournament. So, I used clip art of a golfer on it.

"Brilliant programme you've got here to do these posters" my colleague said as I gave it to him.

"Yes - it will even merge images together - so you could merge the golfer and the maid and have a transvestite golfer!" I replied.

"What's wrong with that?" he demanded in a camp voice and hand on hip!

"Nothing at all, I do it all the time" I answered.

His mouth dropped to the floor as he stared at me.

"No that's not true" I said .... leaving a pregnant pause .... "I haven't played golf in years"

"Nice one!" he exclaimed laughing.

Oh well. Two hours later I was at a Northern Concord meeting dressed and relating the same story!

Photomorph

I was at a presentation of multimedia applications - to demonstrate Photomorph, the presenter had a picture of himself (complete with beard) morph into one of a beautiful girl. He made some comment about cross-dressing!

Afterwards I went up to him and asked about the programme - telling him I wanted to get into the cross-dressing! "You don't need the programme for that" he replied - smiling at my keeping up his joke!

Maybe I don't - but I've been trying to make a sequence exactly as he demonstrated for some time now to show on my pages!

Other incidents

Oh NO!!!!!!

Signs on the motorway indicated road works ahead. I slowed down and kept my distance from the car ahead. As anticipated, the traffic ground to a halt. I stopped well clear of the car ahead, then glanced in my mirror and saw that the car behind me was also going to stop. Unfortunately, I could also see that the one behind her was not going to pull up in time. He hit her and she was knocked into me.

Fortunately, there was not a lot of damage done to my car - it was still driveable with a dent and a broken light bulb.

Equally fortunate, my wife's initials are the same as mine - so I just wrote down the initials and surname and address when exchanging details. The others were more concerned about the more extensive damage done where their cars had collided and were happy to see me go.

Is it? Isn't it?

I called in at a Little Chef (roadside coffee house) while out driving.

There was only one other customer there and two members of staff (one girl one boy - both late teens).

Having taken my order for a drink, the girl went back to the counter. I heard them mumbling and was quite certain it concerned whether or not I was a TV.

The boy brought my coffee over. I had just lit a cigarette and coughed as I said thanks - then made some comment about a cough.

As he returned to the counter I heard him say "Yes it is - she just has a bad cough".

Getting Read

Of course, it doesn't always work that way. I was in a Sainsbury supermarket doing my weekly shopping (I've often shopped dressed) when I noticed people glancing at me and giggles behind my back.

What have I done wrong this morning I wondered - convinced that I was being read (which is comparatively rare for me).

Have I got my wig on back to front? Have I made a mess of my make up?

Then I realised. I was not en femme that day!

Which just goes to show that we can get totally paranoid and that the chances are that looks and giggles that we think are because we have been read are probably nothing at all to do with us.

Remember. People see what they expect to see. In a "normal" environment, this does not include cross-dressers. So, unless you attract attention through inappropriate dress or behaviour, the chances are that you won't even attract a second glance. Confidence is all important - nervousness is suspicious. Being cross-dressed may not attract attention, but the nervousness will - then they might look more closely to try to see why you are nervous.

Knuckle Draggers

A group of us were walking up Canal Street in Manchester as a group of what seemed to be football supporters wandered across the bridge by the Rembrandt. Seeing us, one of them called out "Oi, are you lot men or women?"

I replied: "More of a man than you'll ever be; more of a woman than you'll ever have."

You could almost hear them grunt as their knuckles rubbed along the pavement.

About the author

Helen Dale

Helen identifies as female with a transsexual history - her preferred pronouns are she/ her. She grew up as a RAF Brat and dreamed of being a pilot herself but failed the medical due to having had hay fever (the RAF considered it risky trying to land an aircraft and sneezing at the wrong moment).

Throughout her childhood and early career in pr, advertising and marketing and getting married and having a family, she concealed the secret that she was transgender.

In 1998, Helen accepted that she needed to transition. Losing one job as a consequence, Helen joined Greater Manchester Probation as IT help desk manager in 1999. As the first openly trans employee nationally she provided awareness training for probation and prison staff (and others) and became the de facto lead on trans issues.

Helen persuaded the then Lesbian and Gay staff association (LAGIP) to extend its membership criteria to include trans and bisexual members and spent several years as chair. She also helped to found a:gender - the UK pan-Civil Service trans support network and was made an honorary life member when she retired in 2015.

She served on local and national diversity boards and chaired a trans charity in Manchester as well as training as a counsellor. Her work was recognised with several awards including a Butler Trust Award presented by HRH Princess Anne at Buckingham Palace.

Since retiring, Helen has continued to present workshops on trans issues and provide counselling for trans individuals. She also became a volunteer with Diversity Role Models - going into schools and talking to students about homophobic, transphobic and biphobic bullying.

Overall, Helen estimates that she's met well over 1,000 trans individuals who would previously been described as transsexual and many more who do not plan to transition permanently including cross-dressers, gender fluid, non-binary, drag artists/drag queens and some who identify as she-male. The discussions she's had with all of these individuals mean she has a huge wealth of information to draw on for her stories to ensure that they are authentic.

Helen started writing short stories for Cross Talk, Northern Concord Trans Support Group magazine, in the mid/ late 1990s — and started to write a novel while she was 'between contracts'. That novel was put on hold when she started working for Greater Manchester Probation in 1999.

After surgery in 2000, she joined Spice, a social activity group, in Manchester and did a number of adventurous events with them. This led to her colleagues asking, on Monday mornings, what she'd done at the weekend.

Typical answers were driving a tank, flying a jet, sailing a yacht, riding a quad bike or a hovercraft. Her colleagues told her that she'd led such an interesting life, she should write her autobiography — so she did.

While recollecting memories for it, she recalled an incident when she was 19 and living in London. She'd taken the train to Bournemouth, changing in the toilets at the end of the carriage and crossing over to Studland Bay and sunbathing in a bikini. She realised that she was being watched so left quickly.

But, what if she hadn't noticed the guy?

What if he hadn't minded that she was trans?

That struck her as a possible start of a novel — which became 'Summer Dreams'.

Since retiring, Helen has been a member of the Manchester Women's Writers' Group which has provided valuable feedback on her work.

Please check out Helen's website: www.helendaleauthor.info and join her mailing list or follow her on Facebook at:

https://www.facebook.com/helendaleauthor/

Also by Helen Dale

Summer Dreams

"Summer Dreams" is an authentic story of the transgender community and illustrates the wide range of trans people's experiences, the problems, prejudices and fears that they face (and some of their own prejudices) — and the fact that being trans is just one facet of their lives. It was inspired by a true incident when the author was about 19.

But let Vicky tell you about Summer Dreams:

I was David, but now I'm Vicky.

I was sunbathing in sand dunes near Bournemouth in 2003, when Roger found me and changed my life. After spending a heavenly holiday with him as Vicky, I just couldn't face reverting to David. I knew, though, that becoming Vicky permanently was impossible.

There was only one option, I tried to kill myself.

Roger saved me then showed how life as Vicky was possible.

Summer Dreams tells of my transition journey, coming out to family and friends and their reactions, some of which were very difficult to deal with, especially Peter my twin brother's and the abuse we faced from him and others.

But being trans is just part of who I am. Roger and I have a normal life too.

But is it too good to last?

Summer Dreams is an adult novel with explicit sex scenes

It is set in 2003-8 when the terms transvestite and transsexual were commonly used.

ISBN Paperback   978-1-9996329-3-9

What Readers have said:

"Brilliant"

"LGBT meets Howard's Way"

"A page turner"

"Informs about trans issues without pushing it down the readers throat"

"It's a really good introduction to transgender issues and a romantic novel very well written "

"It's proper steamy, John didn't put it down beginning of lockdown, kept saying his glasses were steaming up"

Changes

A tale of corruption, blackmail, revenge, drug smuggling, murder, and self-discovery told from five points of view:

Nigel Hall has a comfortable life running his advertising agency and using girls and other activities including sailing and trips to casinos to entertain his clients.

George Collins enjoys perks that Nigel gives him and doesn't worry too much about the invoices he approves.

John Ives hadn't expected to take his cousin **Carol Ives**'s part as Cinderella in a panto when she injured her ankle horse-riding nor that photos from the event would later give his fiancée an idea for getting him in and out of her parents' house without their knowledge. Nor did he expect to discover how much he enjoyed cross-dressing or that his fiancée would support him.

Then **Mary Sanchez**, the widow of OJ, a former business partner of Nigel, returns from the USA. She takes over the company George works for and extracts revenge on Nigel, who she blames for OJ's death.

The consequences impact on all of them.

ISBN Paperback   978-1-9996329-6-0

Operation Busted Flush

'"And I say the time for waiting is over. He's tried to stop us serving in the military. He's tried to withdraw rights we've fought for. He wants to prevent us using appropriate washrooms. Now he wants to eliminate us completely – they've even taken down every reference to transgender off government websites for Christ's sakes! Enough is enough. We have to f*****g do something!" Angela slapped her hand on the table.'

A group of ex-special forces transgender veterans decide to take action to defend their community against the White House's attack on transgender people.

ISBN Paperback 978-1-9996329-5-3

What readers say:

"I thoroughly enjoyed this novella. It follows the antics of the President of the USA 2016 to 2020 and his aggressive attitude towards the LGBT community. A group of transgender ex-soldiers vow to take their revenge. I loved the scenes in the cabin where they were plotting with military precision how enact their plan. I was with them all the way. There were also moments of tenderness – planning for a wedding and support for the grieving. I have very little experience of the trans community but now realise how hard they have fought for their rights in society and what a massive impact the attitudes of national leaders have on their everyday lives. A real page turner - I couldn't wait to hear what happened next and it kept you guessing to the very last page."

"Transgender avengers form a crack team to take down a corrupt and authoritarian US president before he causes more harm to their community. Good action-adventure romp with wish fulfilment for all those who have watched in despair over the past years as our hard won trans rights are attacked by governments worldwide. Thoroughly enjoyed it."

A Tale of Two Lives:
A Funny Thing Happened on the Way to the Palace

Inspirational story of award winning trans activist, writer, trainer and counsellor: Helen Dale.

Having grown up as a RAF Brat and keen scout, dreaming of being a pilot in the RAF, she concealed a secret for decades before accepting, in 1998, that she needed to transition.

Losing one job as a consequence, she joined Greater Manchester Probation in 1999. As the first openly trans employee nationally she provided awareness training for probation and prison staff and others and became the de facto lead on trans issues.

She persuaded the then Lesbian and Gay staff association to extend its membership criteria to include trans and spent several years as chair. She also helped to found a:gender — the UK pan-Civil Service trans support network and was made an honorary life member when she retired in 2015. She served on local and national diversity boards and chaired a trans charity in Manchester as well as training as a counsellor.

Her work was recognised with several awards including a Butler Trust Award presented by HRH Princess Anne at Buckingham Palace.

"A Tale of Two Lives" tells how she came out to family and friends and how that might have been handled better! It also covers her life after transition, embarking on a range of activities learning to scuba dive, qualifying as a yacht skipper, fire breathing, diving with sharks — including Great Whites — and holidaying around the world as part of a group or on solo trips showing that being trans is no barrier to living a full life.

ISBN

Paperback:	(b/w illustrations):	978-1-9996329-7-7
Hardcover (colour illustrations):		978-1-9996329-9-1

what readers have said:

"an excellent read and filled in some of the gaps in your eventful life. It was a brave thing to write it but I would not expect anything less from you"

"I've read the book and found it very interesting, down to earth, no holds barred, and for me personally extremely helpful in understanding a close relative in a similar situation. Well done, I look forward to the next one."

"A book about journeys and self-discovery and how to weather life's ups and downs. Fascinating insights into Helen's transition story richly peppered with the fullness of family, friendship, work and really living life to the full. Yes, Helen you have made a difference"

"I really enjoyed this book which covers the very interesting life story of Helen. "It's a really good read and keeps you interested as well as explaining more about the TV/TS community and the struggles they can face. Highly recommended"

"I loved this book and as my son is experiencing some of the same issues it gave me insight. I also bought the book for him which I think helped, though he has chosen not to transition. He chose instead to tell his closest friends and felt able to do that."

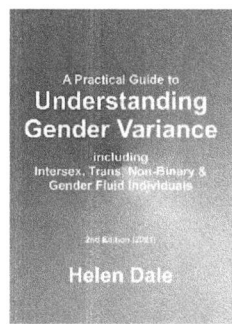

Understanding Gender Variance -
A Practical Guide: including Intersex, Trans, Non-Binary & Gender Fluid Individuals

based on the author's award-winning transgender awareness workshops

Hard cover version includes colour illustrations; paperback version illustrations are black and white.

Helen Dale has been involved in the trans community for more than twenty years; initially providing support on the internet then training as a counsellor and counselling supervisor; chairing trans and LGB&T support groups and providing workshops on trans issues to a range of audiences — and has won several awards for this work.

This guide has been developed from those workshops and her personal experiences supporting other trans individuals. It is intended to be easy to read keeping jargon to a minimum and explaining terms in simple language. The information is laid out in logical sections — with a comprehensive contents section to find relevant details easily.

With the number of individuals identifying as trans, intersex, non-binary or gender fluid doubling about every five years, if you haven't previously met or had dealings with a trans individual, you may well do before long whether as a manager or support worker friend or family. It will help you to identify the questions that you need to ask and how to avoid common mistakes. It will also be a valuable resource for anyone who identifies as transgender, intersex, non-binary or gender fluid.

The book is aimed at anyone dealing with trans people
- Counsellors / Help-line Operators/ Befrienders
- Support/ Social Workers
- Union Staff
- Teachers and Lecturers
- Citizens Advice Bureaux
- Samaritans
- Criminal Justice System staff including
- Equality and Diversity Practitioners
- HR staff
- Other Managers
- LGBT+ organisations
- Family & Friends
- And Trans Individuals themselves

Contents include:
- Definitions
- Causality
- Social Transition

- Transsexual Journey to Surgery
- Travelling on: Post Transition / Surgery
- Trans Issues in Counselling
- Partners and Families
- Case Studies
- Legal History
- Discrimination & Hate Crime/ Incidents
- Employment
- Trans People in the Criminal Justice System
- Bibliography

ISBN

Paperback (B/w illustrations): 978-1-9996329-3-9

Hardcover (colour illustrations): 978-1-9996329-8-4

what readers have said:

"Your books were the first thing I found that made sense from a human point of view instead of science and big words."

www.ingramcontent.com/pod-product-compliance
Lightning Source LLC
Chambersburg PA
CBHW071422070526
44578CB00003B/656